W9-AZR-688

The SECRETS to WRITING A SUCCESSFUL BUSINESS PLAN

A PRO SHARES A STEP-BY-STEP GUIDE TO CREATING A PLAN THAT GETS RESULTS

HAL SHELTON

Summit Valley Press · Rockville, Maryland

ISBN: 978-0-9899460-3-2
ISBN (eBook): 978-0-9899460-4-9

Published by:
Summit Valley Press
P.O. Box 2352
Rockville, MD 20847
www.secretsofbusinessplans.com

Ordering Information: Special discounts are available on quantity purchases of 500 or more copies. To order this book, please visit our website, write to the publisher at Summit Valley Press, P.O. Box 2352, Rockville, MD 20847, or email the author at henry.shelton@scorevolunteer.org.

Editor and Project Manager: Marla Markman, www.MarlaMarkman.com
Book Design: TLC Graphics: www.TLCGraphics.com
Cover: Tamara Dever; *Interior:* Marisa Jackson

Publisher's Cataloging-in-Publication Data

Shelton, Hal, 1943- author.
    The secrets to writing a successful business plan : a
pro shares a step-by-step guide to creating a plan that
gets results/Hal Shelton. —Updated and expanded.
    pages cm
    Includes index.
    LCCN 2016918554
    ISBN 978-0-9899460-3-2
    ISBN 978-0-9899460-4-9
    1. Business planning. 2. Small business.
3. Entrepreneurship.   I. Title.
    HD30.28.S4285 2017   658.4'012
            QBI16-900085

Printed in the United States of America

23 22 21 20 19 18 17   11 10 9 8 7 6 5 4 3 2

For entrepreneurs thinking of starting or growing their small businesses or nonprofits, and especially to the many SCORE clients I have had the pleasure of helping to start and grow their business dreams.

CONTENTS

FOREWORD

It has been three years since this book was first released. After rereading it, I found that Hal's book (and my foreword) have withstood the test of time. It remains an outstanding resource for anyone who aspires to start their own business and develop a business plan. It is also perfect for anyone who has a business, either to make sure they are on the right course or for those who need to hit the "refresh" button by changing and updating their business plan. It is critically important that existing business owners regularly review their plans and results against their business plan. If it is hard to remember to conduct a thoughtful review of your plan or you think you don't have the time, do it when the time changes. Reset your clock, test the batteries in your smoke and carbon monoxide detectors, and review your business plan.

You won't believe how many times during my 20 years as CEO of SCORE I've heard someone say that writing a business plan isn't necessary to a business's success. I've heard all the excuses: "It's a waste of time," "They're outdated," "I've got it all in my head." If they've been saying it's outdated for 20 years, it must be really outdated. But no matter how many decades pass, at the heart of every business are still the same components for success. Analyzing these moving parts before and during business ownership is critical to making sure the result is worthwhile and successful.

I have seen firsthand the effectiveness of business plans every day during my tenure with SCORE—in every new business idea that gets fleshed out, every new storefront that obtains the financing needed to successfully open on Main Streets across the country, and every enterprise whose planned growth adds additional jobs in its community.

Based his experience working with over 1,000 small business clients, Hal Shelton will, and does, concur. This book is a result of Hal's extensive experience and expertise gained from his 11 years as a SCORE mentor, 45 years working in the business and nonprofit sectors, and his dual perspective from having sat on both sides of the investment proposal table. This book is an efficient and effective guide to creating a roadmap that makes sure your business's actions are aligned with the direction you ultimately want to go. One thousand-plus clients later, Hal knows what steps are necessary to achieve success and the most straightforward way to accomplish them. You are now the beneficiary of this wisdom.

Do not think of this book (or the business planning process) as a one-time endeavor. Even once your initial business plan is "complete," it should be reviewed and revised on a continuous basis. As your business evolves, use your plan to make sure you're on track to reaching your goals. As your goals and various aspects of your business change, so too should your business plan. Use this book again and again as a reference guide to keep your plan as relevant and useful as possible.

I'll admit, there are some decisions in life where caution can be thrown to the wind—and the thrill can be exhilarating. Decisions like picking a restaurant for dinner, trying a new sport, or buying a new outfit can be made on a whim with little planning or forethought. But all these decisions have relatively little at stake. When starting or growing your business—your livelihood to which you've likely devoted a great deal of time and money—it's vital to invest the time and forethought in creating a plan that will guide your actions.

Getting started on the path to creating a business plan may seem daunting. But using this book to tackle one section of your business plan at time will make the process easier and guarantee you have a clear picture of every facet of your business.

W. Kenneth Yancey Jr.
Chief Executive Officer
SCORE Association

A NOTE FROM THE AUTHOR

I am gratified with the market's reception to the first edition: The book achieved Amazon bestseller status, and reviews praise the core messages—informative, easy to read, demystifying a complex subject, and helpful to readers' pursuits.

I am also pleased that several college professors (University of Iowa, Purdue, Berkeley, Paul Smith College, Savannah College of Art and Design, and probably some I do not know about) are using the book in their entrepreneurial courses. Students are the next wave of entrepreneurs, and training now will help improve their odds of success.

Friends have encouraged me to write a second book on small business. However, I feel there is unfinished business with the business plan basics, so I have decided to write a second edition. Contributing to this decision are the following points:

- Data included in the first edition is several years old and needs updating.

- Some key funding alternatives have changed, including the ability of all citizens to invest in start-up/early-stage companies, dramatic growth in all types of crowdfunding platforms, and revised SBA-loan guarantee programs.

- Since the original book was written, I have continued with SCORE mentoring and angel investing, so I have more experience and stories to share.

- With more than 10,000 books published, there are many entrepreneurs looking for the next stage of advice: Now that I have started a business, what should I be thinking about?

- I advise entrepreneurs that when your business and markets change, it is time to update your business plan, so I am following my own advice and updating the book.

INTRODUCTION

As a small business mentor, I meet many entrepreneurs who are interested in launching a business, growing a business, or starting a nonprofit. Here are three typical client stories:

Fred came into our mentoring session with a big smile and his laptop fired up. After introductions, I asked how I could help him. He started waving his hands and said with obvious pride that he was quitting his job as a mid-level accountant in a big manufacturing company and was planning to open a bed and breakfast that catered to company off-site meetings in a resort community two hours away. He further mentioned that his goals were to earn $1 million, be his own boss, and set his own schedule. Many thoughts were going through my mind on how to respond to this news, but what I said was, "Do you have a business plan?" I knew that if Fred could write a quality business plan that would convince a bank to lend the $275,000 he needed to buy the B&B, he would realize that, as founder and CEO, he would work for and be subject to the demands and schedules of his customers, employees, vendors, and the weather. In addition, he would see that to be a successful B&B proprietor, he would need passion and persistence, along with a product/service that was differentiated from competitors. I added that a good plan addresses the seemingly perverse question of how you're going to handle unanticipated situations.

Ann told me about the marketing company she founded 20 years ago. She was facing difficult market conditions, and hence cash flow shortfalls, as traditional clients were spending less and finding alternatives for her services, particularly online and offshore. She hoped to continue in the business for another 10 years and then transfer it to her son who worked as a researcher in the company. Ann talked about how the business had changed from when she started it. She was sure she needed a strategic plan but did not know where to start. Again, many thoughts were going through my mind, and I asked her if she had a budget and a vision/goal for where she would like to take the business. I knew that if she had a good grasp on her current situation and a feel for the future, became more comfortable with financial and analytical tools, and learned more about current marketing trends, a business plan process in which Ann would lead and involve her key staff would provide a firm bridge from today to tomorrow.

Bob, Larry, and Barbara were very excited to tell me about their idea of how to share their gospel through song and get paid for their weekend passion of singing at youth groups associated with their church. They would form a nonprofit, receive a salary and benefits, and build equity, and it would all be funded through grants and donations. They already had a lot of experience on the types of music that were of interest. Again, I had many thoughts. I asked how they planned to structure their operation, and they replied they had already agreed among themselves who would hold what position and how decisions would be made. I further asked about their board of directors, and they responded with, "What board of directors?" I knew if we could work together on a business plan, Bob, Larry, and Barbara would learn much about the intricacies and legalities of forming and operating a nonprofit. Among other things, they would learn that a nonprofit's assets/equity do not belong to the founders, it is not the only organizational design for entrepreneurs who want to contribute to their communities, and it has of two sets of customers—the people being served and the people providing the funding. Maybe the way to start was with a feasibility study.

Who This Book Is For

These are three true stories, though the names have been changed. Are you in a similar position of planning to start a business, growing an existing business, or starting a nonprofit? What these entrepreneurs have in common is the need to develop the knowledge and plans to guide them to a successful business launch and operation. While this learning and planning process takes many forms, shapes, and levels of intensity, it is all considered part of the business planning process.

If you are in a situation similar to any of our three stories, this book is written for you. It is for entrepreneurs who are thinking of starting a small business or nonprofit and for small business owners who want to grow an existing business or solve an operating problem. This book will also help if you are looking for assurance that you are headed in the right direction, seeking help with a section of your business plan that you do not understand, feeling that a section of your business plan is not robust enough and want pointers, or wanting to learn where and how to apply for funding. Entrepreneurs should always surround themselves with mentors and advisors, so you will also find ideas on where to find these valuable resources.

IT'S LIKE THIS: A client had started a lawn mowing business two years ago. He had no formal business plan because it was very easy to start this business and there were no barriers to entry. While the business was "paying the bills," the owner wanted to grow the business to become one of the top three landscapers in the local market. He recognized the need for a formal plan to move toward this goal and sought assistance obtaining a bank loan to purchase additional equipment.

Lessons Learned

I have been involved in for-profit businesses and nonprofit organizations for more than 40 years. With this experience and a successful track record, I started mentoring small businesses, and for the past 11 years, I have been with SCORE, a nationwide nonprofit engaged in training, educating, and counseling entrepreneurs to help them start and grow profitable businesses. SCORE was formed in 1964 and has grown to more than 300 chapters. Its business model is based on volunteers, and it has over 10,000 volunteers assisting for-profit and nonprofit entrepreneurs. In 2015, SCORE mentors helped:

- Start 53,377 new businesses

- Create 65,125 jobs (118,502 if you include the founders)

- Increase revenues in 72 percent of established businesses

During my years as a SCORE mentor, I have counseled more than 1,200 entrepreneurs—many of them repeatedly. Also, I am an angel investor, which allows me to be both mentor and investor. Throughout my career, I have either written, presented, or helped others with their business plans. Now I am on the receiving end of entrepreneurs seeking equity financing.

During these SCORE client mentoring sessions and in my angel investments, I have gained firsthand knowledge and have seen what works and what doesn't for entrepreneurs and potential funders. I have seen how entrepreneurs face the challenge of writing a business plan and how intimidating it is to sit down and commit to paper an idea they have been considering for some time. I have also been witness to the mistaken belief entrepreneurs have that every business plan must be exactly like the 30-page, one-size-fits-all templates freely available on many websites rather than adapting these templates to their specific situations. On the contrary, every business plan must answer certain fundamental questions that pertain to your specific business: Who is your audience? Are you writing the business plan for yourself, for others in your organization, or for an external audience? What is your time frame? Do you need external funding? What is your competitive position and strength? What is your value proposition? These and other considerations will shape the design of your business plan. Finally, I have seen the tension the entrepreneur faces when making forecasts—keep it conservative for yourself, but for a potential funder, make it robust so the funder will see this is a good business to invest in or lend to.

The recent "Great Recession" and the slow recovery have been the impetus for many business plans. Many talented people who have been out of work for extended periods and need to generate cash flow are considering starting a business. Smart people with energy and a contribution to make, who never thought of starting their own business, need some place to turn for trusted advice.

While the "Great Recession" may be officially over, many businesses and nonprofits continue to experience cash flow challenges, as the changing economy plays havoc with sales, collections, and donations. Banks have increased their lending standards so small business loans are more difficult to achieve. Even fully collateralized lines of credit with banks that people have done business with for many years are a challenge. These businesses need a way to express their situation and prospects, and often the best venue for this discussion is a business plan. Many small businesses have successfully weathered their first few years and are now poised to grow to the next level; this is another reason to write a business plan.

As the baby boomers reach retirement age, they are considering what new challenges to take on and how to help society. Sitting in a rocking chair on the front porch in a year-round pleasant climate is not an option or a desire for many baby boomers. They are considering forming nonprofits that tap the skills they have learned over a career; it is their time to "give back."

How This Book Is Structured

The book is organized into four sections. The first section will help you gain a good understanding of what a business plan is and is not about, where to find help, how to get started, and some do's and don'ts. The second section gets down to the core of writing the plan, devoting a chapter to exploring each of the main elements of the business plan in detail. The third section covers the all-important topic of raising money by exploring methods of obtaining funding. Finally, the fourth section contains topics of interest to established business owners, but start-up entrepreneurs should read these as well to see what lies ahead and get prepared.

Along the way, you'll find "It's Like This" boxes—real-life examples that I and my SCORE mentor colleagues have encountered during our many years of mentoring. These examples illustrate the topic being discussed (of course, identities and proprietary information have been protected). At the end of each chapter, you will find a summary of "Key Lessons." Throughout the book, there are many references to websites for additional information; please be alert that website addresses change, so you might need to search for the organization if the URL is outdated.

Lastly, recognizing that adults like to learn in increments and have all the information about a subject at hand, I have included everything in the relevant chapter and have not used appendices. Therefore, you do not need to read the book in one sitting. You can read a section at a time, put the book down, and come back—in essence, this will be your reference source. As learning is better achieved through interaction, you will gain more from the material if you think about, research, and make notes as you progress through the chapters. That's why there's a worksheet at the end of each chapter titled "Your Turn," where you can write your thoughts. By the end of the book, collect your comments, and you will have a good start to your business plan. In this manner, you will write your business plan incrementally rather than trying to tackle the whole plan at one time. The "Your Turn" worksheets are also available to complete online or to download from the SCORE website (visit www.score.org/secrets_business_plan).

To make this discussion a reasonable size, I have kept the focus on preparing a business plan in a logical manner, with enough information to provide an appreciation of what needs to be included and the options you may consider. For the details, I trust you will use reference books and material freely available on many websites. For example, I do not address how to hire, fire, and pay employees; obtain vendors; develop a manufacturing plan; do accounting; secure a patent; and so on. All these subjects are covered in a business plan, but you need to do your homework in these areas to gain enough knowledge so you can put together a reasonable plan. However, in areas where I have found the reference material lacking or entrepreneurs have many questions, I have provided more information. For instance, I have included details on how to structure your company with implications for filing taxes, marketing, and financial reporting.

Hal's 12 Commandments for Writing a Business Plan

Through my experience with writing and reading business plans and investing in ventures based on these business plans, I have developed knowledge and opinions on what makes an effective business plan. Following are my 12 Commandments for writing a business plan; I will continually come back to these themes throughout the book.

1. **A business plan is a marketing action.** A well-thought-out and presented business plan demonstrates to yourself and others that you are serious about your business idea, you have the passion and persistence to develop the strategies and tactics so your business idea will be successful, and you have converted a general idea into a realistic and believable business.

2. **Know your audience, and write the plan in a style and with information they need for the action(s) you want them to take.**

To achieve the decisions and actions you wish taken, you must provide your readers with the information in a style they are familiar with and can understand. Maybe this is your banker, angel investor, biggest client, prospective employee or board member, or just yourself. Make it easy for readers to take positive actions—make your case in their language.

3. **Business planning should focus on the customer, not on the entrepreneur.** For-profit businesses and nonprofits alike are established to fulfill a customer/client/society need. The better the need is served or problem solved, the more successful the entity can be. Therefore, focus on satisfying the customer/client need and demonstrating how you are doing it uniquely from the competition.

4. **A small business is usually a bet on the entrepreneur, so provide a biography that demonstrates you have the technical and leadership experience to drive your idea to success. Either demonstrate you have the experience or you have surrounded yourself with others who have it.** Financiers, a personal friend, a stern banker, or a demanding angel know they are investing in you as the owner. You are contributing most of the "assets"—your time, talents, and passion for birthing this business idea into the marketplace. Your biography, therefore, should not be just a LinkedIn-type listing of your education and previous positions. Instead, make the case for why you are the right person at the right time to own, lead, and operate this business.

5. **The executive summary is the most important plan section. It delivers the message and sets the tone. It should be enthusiastic, concise, professional, and no more than two pages long.** Just as in the first few paragraphs of any book, many people will not read past the opening section if they lose interest. In these first two pages, you need to convince the reader that this business idea will be successful

by describing what customer needs are being fulfilled, how this business idea sets itself apart from all the other competing alternatives in the marketplace, and the financial and other rewards to be obtained. Focus on writing this compelling short story in two pages or less. As a summary, it should be written last; this ensures it represents the full plan.

The second commandment was about knowing your reader, and one place this comes into play is in the executive summary. You might have different versions, depending on who the reader is. For example, a banker may be more interested in the stability and reliability of projected cash flows while an angel investor may more interested in market penetration and sales growth.

6. **Have sales goals that are supported by research and an actionable marketing plan.** This is your first and most important sales job. Where and how are you going to capture revenue? Describe your sales revenue goals, make a convincing argument, and provide tangible support—names of first prospects, sales pitch, competitive analysis, market awareness, and so on. If the argument and support are not convincing, then the banker, angel investor, vendor, or customer will arbitrarily give the sales goals a "haircut," which will result in a decrease in cash flow (and maybe doom their investment participation)—and you will not be in the room to defend your analysis.

7. **Request funding in the amount you truly need, and support your request with financial statements.** A funding request supported by financial statements (cash generation and expenditures) demonstrates you have thoroughly thought through the business and you consider the financial aspects important. This provides some assurance that you will look out for the best interests of those providing funding.

8. **Use of funding proceeds should be primarily for marketing, sales, and product development activities that will generate the products, services, and sales.** Investors assume you will contribute "sweat equity." While some of the funding may be needed for critical staff salaries, the majority should be used for activities that will generate sales. A growing sales pattern with positive net margins means you will have the cash flow to pay back loans and eventually have a sellable business. Examples of typical funding requests are for protectable/proprietary software development, product production equipment, and marketing programs with a direct or channel partner sales focus.

9. **Surround yourself with advisors and mentors, and talk through your business ideas with them.** Starting and growing a business is difficult, and more than half of all startups fail in their first five years. No one person can have all the knowledge, experience, or even perspective to handle every business situation. Gain from the skills and experiences of others. Ask for advice from similar companies in different geographic markets or noncompeting suppliers in your same market segment. Talk with experts in areas such as marketing, sales, finance, and operations. Join industry groups or entrepreneur mastermind teams. Express your questions and roadblocks, and then listen openly. You will feel less isolated and confused, and investors will feel confident you have a complete team of resources to grow the business. Often, family and friends are not able to provide the kind of feedback and advice you need. Some people find it difficult or do not know how to ask for help; just try it, and you will be pleasantly surprised how willing others are to assist.

10. **A business plan is never perfect and never finished, so do not procrastinate writing it or obsess about creating the ideal plan. At some point, you need to stop writing**

and start satisfying a customer need and making money. Set a personal deadline, stop planning, and get to work.

11. **It *is* all about the money.** Every decision and action you take will have a financial impact—be it cash flow or profit. While many entrepreneurs have multiple bottom lines (lifestyle, mission, causes they believe in, and so on), if you do not have sufficient financial resources, you will not be able to accomplish your mission and goals, or even stay in business. Sometimes this singular fact helps cut through the fog of what to focus on next.

12. **Focus, Focus, Focus.** You will triple the value of your plan and dramatically improve your credibility with a potential funder if you can answer these three questions clearly and thoroughly both in your text and financials:

    a. What are the three to five Critical Success Factors (CSFs), or keys to success, on which you are going to focus most of your time and attention in "getting them right"?

    b. What are the three to five goals (objectives) you are going to achieve over the next 12 to 18 months? They should be tied to the CSFs. Spell them out this way: SMART goals (Specific, Measurable, Action-Oriented, Realistic, and Time-Bound).

    c. What are the strategies you are going to follow to achieve your SMART goals? What are the steps, processes, actions, and milestones, and who is responsible for making it happen? For every goal, there must be measurable action steps for achieving it.

A Book of a Different Color

At Amazon there are hundreds of business plan books. My initial thoughts were, Does the market need another book in this space?

The more I thought about it, the more I decided that with my unique background, I could add insights and examples not provided by others. I fully understand that every business decision you make has a financial impact and affects your cash flow.

Even with hundreds of business planning books available, start-up success rates are not improving, so the message needs to be delivered in a different way. What differentiates this book from competing titles is that it offers practical, actionable advice that is grounded in the reality of my having prepared hundreds of business plans. It is not just academic, and it is not overly focused on the mechanics of filling out the forms, such as those books that provide a template or CD. Here you will find a good balance of the why and the how, along with stories from a long, successful track record.

So, without further ado, let's get started by having you fill out the first of the "Your Turn" worksheets.

YOUR TURN

List four reasons you are reading this book and what you hope to achieve:

1.

2.

3.

4.

BUSINESS PLAN BASICS

In this section, you will discover what a business plan is and why you need to write one, best practices that should be consulted both before and after you write your business plan, and information on where to get help (much of which is free) with preparing your business plan.

Chapter 1

BUSINESS PLANS 101

*What Is a Business Plan
and Why Do You Need One?*

Many consider a business plan to be a formal document containing five key elements: 1) business goals, 2) the reasons why these goals are attainable, 3) a plan for reaching those goals, 4) data backing the uniqueness of the products and services to be sold, and 5) supporting information about the organization and team attempting to reach those goals.

A business plan is comprised of these elements, but it is much more than a physical document; it is a structured process to test ideas to determine if they are feasible and financially attractive. Viewed this way, a business plan becomes a road map to successful implementation of the business idea. This road map then morphs into tactical plans and budgets. During the process of developing a business idea, you develop a consistent set of messages, based on facts and analysis, describing your business idea, which will be used in discussions with funders, investors, customers, board members, advisors, vendors, and employees.

Some events that trigger the need to write a business plan include:

1. Starting a new business (the classic reason)

2. Growing an existing business through new products, new channels, and/or new markets

3. Acquiring a business or franchising your existing business

4. Exiting from the business and the need to provide potential buyers with information about the company. They will be interested in the past as a benchmark, but as you have already reaped the benefits of these accomplishments, potential buyers are interested in the future as you see it. What is the potential they may buy into?

What It Is Not

Now you know what a business plan is and what it is used for. But what is the flip side? Clearly, a business plan is not a guarantee that your business idea will be successful or that you will be able to obtain funding. Since most of the information is forward-looking, it will only be as good as the assumptions used, and if the idea is not well packaged and supported in the business plan, some readers might have different perceptions of these forecasts.

When you do a web search on why you should write a business plan, in many cases, fear is invoked that if you do not have a professionally prepared business plan, you will incur the wrath of the banks and possibly regulators. Many times this type of draconian advice comes from sites that want to sell you a business plan template, write the plan for you, or sell you a book. The reality is that two-thirds of start-ups do not seek third-party funding, so the plan is likely written for yourself and can be of whatever quality you think appropriate. However, the more attention you give to the plan and the planning process, the more that potential weaknesses can be identified and mitigations put in place, so the better your chances of business success.

Are We Done Yet?

A business plan is ever evolving. It is never finished, just as your business is not static. Your goals and approaches change as your business changes. However, this is no excuse not to write a business plan. If you are starting a business in an area in which you are unfamiliar, you might start with a feasibility plan, which is a toned-down business plan, to test the idea and to gain experience in the area. You will be amazed at how much the original idea changes as you become more familiar with the business.

Conversely, a person can become obsessed with writing a business plan—always striving for perfection. But there is no such thing as a perfect business plan. At some point, you have to stop planning and start working. Remember the old axiom "analysis paralysis"—don't do it. If you are a start-up and are still working on your business plan after two months of concentrated effort or six months with part-time attention, then you need to examine your process and get some help or change your helpers. Maybe you are not sufficiently focused, do not have enough industry experience, have hit some walls, or do not have the time or energy to be a business owner right now. If you are in business, your ideas for growth or issue resolution are probably current events, and as time is money, you need to implement the changes quickly to not miss a market opportunity or preserve your cash flow.

Sometimes aiming for perfection leads to very rigid plans and forecasts. Your business and the market are ever changing, so you need some flexibility, maybe a "plan B," just in case. See Chapter 25, "Limber Up," for an in-depth discussion on maintaining some flexibility.

Who Is a Business Plan Written For?

Although most people think the goal of business plans is to seek funding, ultimately, a business plan is written primarily for yourself—

to help you decide whether or not to start or grow a business, to set goals and benchmarks, to use the process for developing a set of compelling and consistent messages describing your business and why you will be successful, and to understand the two roles you have as owner and employee. To amplify these points, as a business owner, you have been thinking about a product or service and how it will satisfy a customer need with much of your focus on market dynamics. When you put together a business plan and its financial section, you will determine if these ideas are financially viable. When you put together the operating, marketing, and organization business plan sections, you will better understand everything involved with running the business and if this is what you really want to do. A good business plan is much more than an assembly of independent fact finding and analysis; it integrates all business aspects and clarifies how one part affects the other:

1. Your executive summary will include succinct statements defining your business, what customer need you are satisfying, how your product or service is different from the competition, and why you will be successful.

2. The operational and financial forecasts you build into your business plan will be your first set of targets, which you will measure your actual results and accomplishments against. Through your research of competitive practices, you will benchmark your forecasted results against industry norms.

3. In your small business, you most likely will have two distinct roles and receive two types of financial compensation—as an employee for which your labor should be appropriately compensated and as an owner receiving a return on the invested capital and risks of being in business. Each of these relationships should be addressed in your business plan and in your determination of the feasibility and viability of your business idea. At the beginning, it is common for both these roles to have no or small monetary rewards.

IT'S LIKE THIS: A personal trainer with much recognition started his own company using a fitness methodology he had developed and branded. When he wrote his business plan and started to understand all the things he would be involved with besides working with clients, especially marketing and the need to solicit business (with the many rejections this brings), he realized that owning a business was not for him.

While this example is about a personal trainer, it also applies to many other fields. In companies with employees, roles can be assigned to match skills and interests. However, in a start-up, the entrepreneur is often performing all the roles and taking all the responsibility.

IT'S LIKE THIS: A client, encouraged by family and friends, planned to sell foreign-made, relatively low-priced handicrafts in the United States. In writing her business plan, she realized the complexity of the import/export business, including arranging for on-site quality-control inspections, packaging, freight forwarding, trade letters of credit, payment terms and banking, customs, and so much more. These activities were of no interest to her, since she was skilled in sales. So she put aside forming her own company and went to work for a large import/export company as its sales manager.

As a small business owner, you are or soon will be working 60 to 100 hours a week and still not getting everything done. If you will be working this hard, you want to make sure it will be worth the effort. Again, this is where a business plan comes in. In the process of developing a business plan, you use research, analysis, and estimates to project future results. If you follow your assumptions and obtain the projected results, will you like the answer? For example, if you project that you will earn $20,000 a year, is that good news? It is good that the number is positive; however, if you live in a large city, have family financial obligations, and are paying off bills and saving for retirement, and plan to make this your full-time activity, it is unlikely you will be satisfied with $20,000. Wouldn't it be good to know this before you invested too much in a business?

A secondary reason to prepare a business plan is to demonstrate that you are serious about starting a business and the activity is not a hobby. According to IRS regulations (section 183 of the tax code), as long as you generated profit in three of the past five years, it is a business; otherwise the IRS may claim it is a hobby. If this occurs, all revenues received continue to be taxable, but your expense deductions are limited. As many start-ups have losses in the early years, you need to protect self if there is an IRS audit.

Business Plan Myths

Following are three popular myths about business plans:

1. **Once written, it does not need to be updated.** On the contrary, your business plan is probably out of date the day after it is written. This is due to the changing nature of business, competitors' actions and reactions, changing market conditions, use of estimates, your accomplishments, and your desires to take the next steps. (See Chapter 24, "A Second Look," for a more in-depth discussion of when is the best time to review your business plan.)

2. **Every business plan has the same format and is 30 pages long.** This is the template found on many websites. But it is inaccurate. There are effective two-page, graphics-centered business plans that are used for established businesses that want to focus on a particular area, like marketing, and need to make sure goals and action plans are aligned. Also, a one-person service business, which does not need third-party funding, may only need a business plan that is no longer than 10 pages and focuses on the messages and marketing. Fred, Ann, and Bob, the trio who wanted to

start a nonprofit in the introduction, will also have a distinct type of business plan, since they have different situations and needs.

3. **A 30-page business plan with lots of financial information will get the bank loan needed to start or grow a business.** A business plan is just one of several criteria for getting a banker to review your loan application. Other criteria, and probably with as much weight, are your personal credit score, your ability to collateralize the loan, providing about 20 to 25 percent of the needed capital, and having projected cash flow about 1.3 times the annual debt service. In addition, if your two-page executive summary is not well done, your banker might not read any further. Likewise, a 10-page PowerPoint presentation supported by a 30-page business plan is no guarantee you will receive angel funding.

A business plan is divided into chapters and sections. Visually, the business planning process looks like this:

Key Lessons

✓ A business plan is primarily written for yourself.

✓ While the business plan is written for you, it should not be about you— it should be about the market and your customers.

✓ A business plan is both a document and a process.

✓ A business plan needs to be tailored to your specific situation and kept current.

✓ A business plan is a necessary step but not a guarantee for obtaining funding.

YOUR TURN

List three thoughts and concerns you have about preparing and using a business plan. Keep these nearby, and hopefully, they will be addressed during the course of this book.

1.

2.

3.

List one to three reasons you are considering writing a business plan.

1.

2.

3.

Chapter 2

WHAT'S YOUR STYLE?

Finding What Type of Plan
Is Right for You

Maybe the first business plans were written on clay tablets by the ancient Sumerians, when they were writing about trading and livestock; but the originator of the modern-day business plan is often credited as Pierre Samuel du Pont de Nemours.

Here's the short story: Before Samuel and his son Éleuthère Irénée left their native France in 1799 to build a gunpowder mill in Delaware, they wrote numerous letters to potential investors that offered a plan on how the mill would make money. Clearly, this was a business plan that worked. Samuel and his son secured their investors, and today their business is known as the DuPont Co.

Today's business plan styles range from informal, back-of-the-envelope sketches to two-page, near-term road maps to 30-page plans with illustrations and exhibits. Which style you choose depends on a number of factors, but common to all styles is a clear message.

Start-Up Business Plans

For a simple start-up requiring no third-party funding, create a short, 10-page informal plan to first convince yourself that the idea is feasible and financially viable, then use it to possibly convince friends and family who are usually the first round of support and funding. If the plan is just for you, then you do not have to include all the things you know, such as your form of organization, contact information, organizational chart, graphics, and a lengthy bio. As with a GPS system in your car, you do not have to be reminded how to leave your neighborhood. However, you should include your marketing plan, a shortened version of your bio, a financial summary in a format that will help you track your business performance, and the important message of what differentiates your product or service from the competition—what customer problem you are solving that is not already provided by the competition. Bob, Larry, and Barbara followed this approach, first starting with a feasibility study described later in Chapter 6, including the specifics for nonprofits outlined in Chapter 15.

If you are a start-up seeking bank or equity funding, you will want a formal, lengthy plan tending toward the stereotyped 30-page model. Start with a simpler version, and expand it as your idea matures through experience from talking with others in the field, finding a mentor to discuss key issues with, and talking with potential funders on what they look for and require. Speak with potential customers about what they are looking for in a product/service and how they go about making a buying decision. Include all the items discussed in the simple plan mentioned above. Remember Fred from the introduction—he took this approach in developing his B&B business plan.

Plans for Existing Businesses

For established businesses, start with a short plan, emphasizing mission and goals, to ensure the venture is headed in the right direction for the next year. If you are planning to grow your business, focus on markets, products, and services, in addition to having sufficient resources and any necessary funding. If you are solving an operating issue, focus on that particular matter, such as staffing, cash flow (expense reduction, collections, pricing), operations, vendors, etc. Ann, mentioned in the introduction, followed this approach for her marketing company, focusing on customer needs and her staff resources to assist customers, including her employees' knowledge and experience of current marketing best practices.

Let's look at a practical example of a brief, but focused, business plan for an existing business. An existing business that is focusing on increasing sales may determine after talking with its customers, assessing its competition, and conducting research that it needs to enhance the awareness of its products and services in the marketplace and, in particular, the online marketplace. In this situation, a two-page business plan might be ideal for focusing on marketing and the connection between objectives, goals, initiatives, and actions. This type of plan can be presented in an all-graphic layout that might look like this:

Objectives:

One objective might be "Everyone knows we are here to provide quality products and services." A second objective could be "Our customers are fully satisfied with their purchases."

Goals:

For the first objective of "Everyone knows we are here to provide quality products and services," two goals might be: 1) Boost social media 50 percent, email open rates 20 percent, and email click-thru rates 20 percent; and 2) increase media reach 10 percent and conduct a brand awareness survey that shows strong, positive results.

Initiatives:

For the first goal of "Boost social media 50 percent, email open rates 20 percent, and email click-thru rates 20 percent, two initiatives might be: 1) Manage online content, and 2) get the word out via media channels.

Action Plans:

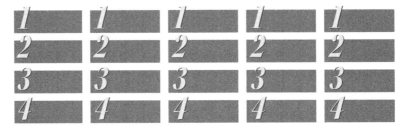

For the first initiative of "Manage online content," the action plans in this situation might be: 1) Leverage blogs and current content, 2) write or revise a social media plan, and 3) increase multimedia content.

This short, graphics-based plan is designed so each objective has one or more goals, each goal has one or more initiatives, and each initiative has one or more action plans. Reading from the bottom up answers the "why" question. And reading from the top down answers the "how" question.

For established businesses seeking funding from existing bank sources, use a medium-sized plan in the 7- to 15-page range. Talk with your small business loan officer (this is probably a different person from the branch manager) and see what he/she requires from someone the bank already knows. If seeking equity funding through an angel or angel group, talk with them about their requirements. For angels, you will eventually need all the information contained in the formal 30-page-plus plan but usually not at the outset. Initially, they will probably prefer to see a three- to five-page bullet point "pitch presentation," which will allow them to assess their initial interest.

Plan-as-You-Go Business Plan

Another approach to business planning is to plan as you go. We have all heard stories of the college student who, having no business experience of any kind, creates a product/service in his dorm room or parents' garage and becomes a multimillionaire. These are rare instances and are not the recommended path for most of us to follow. The positive takeaway, though, is the notion that a business plan is dynamic and you should be making adjustments as you implement your plan and learn from the results.

Meeting Expectations

Most business plans have an executive summary at the beginning and financial statements at the end. In the middle are many sections that describe the business idea and provide the data for developing the financial forecasts. You have the flexibility to arrange this discussion in a logical manner that best describes the company and its operation. There is no rule that says a business plan must be prepared in a particular way. However, if you use a format/design very different from what your audience is used to, they may find it too difficult or time consuming to read your plan. Make it organized, clear, and purposeful.

It helps to know your audience and what information they need to act favorably on your funding request. For example, a banker wants to know how much money is requested, what it will be used for, how long the funding is needed for, and reasonable projections that you will have the resources to repay the loan in full. Hence they focus on the financial statements. An angel investor wants to know that the business can grow and there is an exit strategy in three to five years when he/she can achieve a three- to five-times return. Angel investors and venture capitalists focus on many things, but number one is the entrepreneur and his/her management team—do they have the experience and capability to lead and substantially grow this company to success over several years?

Visual business plans—with lots of charts and pictures—are a relatively new trend. This might be a good approach to help you visualize the entirety of your business idea, but traditional funding sources are not yet into these types of formats. Using charts and graphs in a traditional business plan format is a good idea, as they are visually pleasing and sometimes a picture is worth a thousand words. However, make sure the subject of the graph or chart is worth showing and it tells a compelling message. As we will see, a good executive summary is a maximum of two pages, so there is no room for frivolous charts in this section.

Common to all business plan styles is having a clear message—the elevator pitch. Be able to explain clearly and succinctly what customer problem you are solving, why your solution is better than current alternatives, what tasks are necessary for the business to succeed, what the value is to investors, and, most important, why you will be successful. Some people call these statements the "value proposition," used by you to focus your marketing approach and by lenders and funders to determine if you have a clear understanding and path forward for your business.

Key Lessons

- ✓ Design your business plan in a manner that best demonstrates and explains your business idea.

- ✓ Know your audience and what information in what style they need to act favorably.

- ✓ The message is more important than the style.

YOUR TURN

Given your particular situation and reasons for writing your business plan (which you listed at end of the previous chapter), now list your audience, what you would like them to do after reading your business plan, and what information they need to favorably take that action. Hint: The audience could be you, a banker, an angel investor, a key vendor, a potential employee, a contracting official, etc.

AUDIENCE	ACTION TO BE TAKEN	INFORMATION NEEDED

As you are writing your business plan, refer back to this chart from time to time to ensure you stay focused and on message.

Chapter 3

THE 4-1-1

Where to Go for Business Plan Help

To write or not to write the business plan yourself and where to find information and resources to help you out if you choose to tackle it on your own is the focus of this chapter.

The "Write" Move?

Of course, the ultimate in help is to have someone write your business plan for you. Simply do a web search for "someone to write my business plan," and you will receive hundreds of offers to write your plan by people who claim to have experience in your industry. Of course, they offer testimonials from satisfied clients, all communications will be by email and phone, and the cost will range from $2,000 to $20,000.

However, getting a ghostwriter for your business plan is not generally the best idea. While you might get a good-looking document and it will involve less sweat equity, you will have not been through the process, which was mentioned earlier as the true benefit. Without your input, it will be a canned write-up anyone can use, which will not take into consideration your unique situation or what competitive advantages you might have or need to profitably take business away from competitors. If you are going to supply all the information, you might as well write the plan yourself. An exception to the no-ghostwritten rule is if you need a big, formal plan to secure funding and you are not proficient in English; in that case, hire someone to help you edit the plan, but you better understand everything it contains.

IT'S LIKE THIS: A client wanted to enter the retail food business market with a secret family recipe that had been well tested at family gatherings and a few catering opportunities. He realized he had limited business experience, so he found a marketing professional whom he thought might be a partner, and she developed the business plan. However, it was clear in discussions he did not know that the plan contained a market-entry point different from his thinking and he had no comprehension of the assumptions used to generate the financial statements. While this was slightly embarrassing, it would have been fatal in meetings with potential funders.

This delegating to someone else to write your business plan also occurs within an organization.

IT'S LIKE THIS: A CEO who spent all his time with potential clients gave his COO the task of preparing the business plan. The COO prepared a great plan following all the guidelines, but, as the COO says, "Unfortunately, as well as we worked together, my plan was not exactly his plan, and this sometimes embarrassed him in presentations as he had not taken the time to review what I had written."

DIY Business Planning

If you choose to write your own business plan a lot of help is available. For free face-to-face mentoring assistance, try these sources:

1. **SCORE at www.score.org.** Click on "Find Your Local Chapter," and enter your ZIP code, or scroll down the page. If the locations cited appear too far away, call and see if they have a branch office closer to you. If it's still too far, click on "Find a Mentor" and then "Communications Options" to find a mentor whom you can work with via email. In addition to mentoring, SCORE offers online and in-person workshops, webinars, podcasts, templates, blogs, and tips on many start-up and small business subjects.

2. **Small Business Administration at www.sba.gov.** The SBA website has pertinent information about starting a business and doing business with the federal government.

3. **Small Business Development Centers at www.asbdc-us.org.** In the "Get Started" block, enter your ZIP code.

4. **Women's Business Centers** (about 100 centers nationwide, serving both women and men): Find the one closest to you at www.sba.gov/content/womens-business-centers-directory-0.

As stated in the book's introduction, the internet is a 24/7 reference source—use it. Go to Amazon.com or another book seller, and in the books category, type in something like "how to start a [put in the type of business you want to start or are in]." Since virtually every type of business has already been started by someone else, this search will almost always produce a number of results. After looking at each book's table of contents, you will find one or two that seem potentially helpful. Buy one or two used, and for about $10, you can get a couple of books that will be of great help. The 50-plus titles in the *Business Start-up Guide Series*, published by Entrepreneur Press, are an excellent source of industry information. They can be ordered on Amazon.com or directly through Entepreneur.com, or some SCORE offices have them to lend.

Another idea is to use a search engine like Google or Yahoo; in the search field, type in "Free Business Plan for [put in the type of business you want to start or are already in]." If you do not find a business plan exactly like what you need, you will find some that are close. Focus on how the author developed the content rather than the multicolored pie charts and graphs. Your mission is to learn from someone who has been down this road before, not to copy.

Finally, many companies that are interested in attracting small business customers have content on their websites to cater to the small business market. They do not just provide information about the company's products and services but how to start and operate a successful business. Check out websites from financial institutions, credit card processors, and supply companies of many types. One company that is focused on helping small businesses is Deluxe Corp. You might know them as producers of bank checks, but now they do much more with information on brand identity, email marketing, social media management, and more. Another example of a large company thinking small is American Express, with their American Express Open program focused on small businesses. GrowBiz Media is a small business providing news, trends, tool kits, and information to other small businesses on its SmallBizDaily website (www.smallbizdaily.com). You will also find good information on The UPS Store website, as it caters to many small business customers.

Once you have your mentoring in place and relevant industry information, you can plug it into your business plan. Business plan templates are helpful for guiding you step by step through the writing process. If you are looking for a business plan template, a general internet search will pull up hundreds. In fact, if you go to SCORE for help, mentors will often refer you to and work with you in the organization's templates. To find the free templates, go to www.score.org/resources/business-plans-financial-statements-template-gallery. In conjunction with obtaining assistance from SCORE or another resource, some

entrepreneurs buy either LivePlan or Business Plan Pro, both by Palo
Alto Software (www.paloalto.com/business_plan_software/).

Key Lessons

✓ However the business plan is put together—by you, by others, or as a
team effort—make sure you know what is in the plan and understand
the content and nuances, especially if you are applying for financing
and you face a Q&A session from the lender or investor.

✓ The internet is your library. Use it, and learn from others who have
gone down this road before you.

✓ Take advantage of free services offered by SCORE, SBDC, and other
organizations that focus on helping entrepreneurs to be successful.

List at least two resources you will contact to receive assistance with writing your business plan or at least bounce ideas off of to get another perspective.

	RESOURCE	TELEPHONE NUMBER	EMAIL ADDRESS
1.			
2.			
3.			
4.			

List at least two books and/or websites you will read/visit to gain more knowledge about your business idea.

	BOOK AND/OR WEBSITE
1.	
2.	
3.	
4.	

MAKE NO MISTAKE

Common Business Plan Writing Errors

When writing your business plan, be wary of the common mistakes entrepreneurs make. Depending on the intended use of the plan, these errors can be fatal, especially if you are seeking funding. But more important, these mistakes may result in not providing yourself with the right information and thus you may reach the wrong decision regarding the implementation of your business idea. One of the reasons for writing a business plan is to confirm your business idea is valid and will result in a successful business. If you do not have the right information, you may fool yourself into believing your idea is a winner. These mistakes are organized by business plan sections. Use this list both at the beginning of writing your business plan as a thought-provoker and as a final step in comparing your business plan to best practices.

Executive Summary and General Layout

- **The opening message does not succinctly describe the business idea and why it will be successful.** A full plan is often judged by its two-page executive summary, so first impressions are most important. This mistake often appears as an extensive discussion about the product's engineering, with limited mention of marketing, management capabilities, or expected financial results. Another variation is having a number of charts that do not convey a key message and just take up space. Bankers, investors, and important vendors are busy people, so upon a quick read of this section, if they sense there is not a fit, they will move to the next proposal.

- **The business plan layout reflects poorly on the entrepreneur.** A business plan should be laid out in a logical manner. It should be easy to find items through a table of contents, and the page numbers, spelling, and grammar must be correct. There should not be much repetition of ideas/words, fluff, or tangential comments. The business plan itself is a marketing tool and should mirror the quality effort you will give to your business.

- **The business plan focuses on you and not what you are doing for potential customers.** Businesses are successful when they provide products and services that satisfy a customer need and do it profitably. You start a business because you are good at what you do and are passionate about it. You may also have theories about how business should be conducted, but the focus needs to be on the customer.

IT'S LIKE THIS: A client had a goal to move to the Bahamas. Granted, this might be a reward for being successful, but the goal/dream needs to concentrate on the business, solving a customer need, and demonstrating your passion for it. Focusing on generating income to enable him to travel in style will cause the client to miss what potential customers' needs are.

IT'S LIKE THIS: A client had an idea for a web-based social network centered around his hobby where customers on subscription could chat about new products, events, and more related to the hobby. Client planned to build a facility to test new products and conduct demos. The facility would also include a rooftop residence—both of which were in a resort town in another state. The plan really seemed to be all about trying to have a personal residence paid for as a business expense. The approach should have been to start with a focus on the customer.

General Company Description

- **Key information is hidden.** Hiding key information like commitments, guarantees, funding from other sources, legal issues, and so on is a no-no. A financier needs to fully understand where in the line of repayment/reward he/she stands. If this information is not clearly laid out by the entrepreneur and found through prospective funder due diligence, it will probably kill the deal.

Products and Services

- **There is no focus on particular products and services.** Starting a business is hard and generating cash flow is difficult, so often entrepreneurs will, in effect, say they will do whatever the client wants as long as they pay. There is a natural tension at first to do whatever is necessary to generate cash flow, but this is not a good strategy since it is hard to message and market being all things to all customers. This mistake is similar to the marketing consultant who says they will devise a new product offering strategy for any size company in every market on every continent.

- **Not enough emphasis is placed on the current business and its challenges.** Sometimes entrepreneurs get so caught up in their own enthusiasm of what the business may become, they spend too much ink discussing growth, expansion, franchising, international branches, and other details—all several years down the road. While there is a place for discussing the dream, most of the plan should be focused on the current business and its challenges, such as initial funding, product development, branding, product distribution, and staffing. Financiers, vendors, and other interested parties want to be sure you are focused.

Marketing

- **There is no understanding of the market.** What is the market for your products and services? A red flag for a funder is the claim of no competition—every business has competition. Another red flag is to say the market potential is $1 billion, with no supporting information. If applying for equity financing from angels or venture capitalists, demonstrate the potential for a large market and that the company is scalable to meet this demand.

- **There is no clear statement on how you will generate revenue.** Not only do you need to clearly communicate with the reader about how you will generate revenue—sometimes called the business model—but often, and especially when applying for a bank loan, the small business loan officer will have to communicate with the loan approver. So make sure the reader "gets it."

- **The sales forecast is not believable.** The sales forecast needs to be supported by data and analysis, a marketing plan that will find prospects and convert them to customers, and a discussion of competitor reaction to a new market entrant. Sales forecasts that start off modestly and then dramatically upswing need much justification. The problem with these types of unsupported forecasts is that the reader discounts them and moves on, and you are not in the room to defend your methodology.

- **The plan demonstrates a large amount of hubris.** Many marketing sections lack a concrete actionable plan. Instead, the entrepreneur seems to believe that miraculously, by word of mouth, customers will find their business and buy their fabulous product or service, without any efforts to drive this traffic to their door. Your great product or service is what brings back repeat business; therefore, you need a specific marketing plan to identify and attract new customers.

Management Team and Organization

- **Key player bios are not included.** Small business is most often a bet on the entrepreneur since the business does not have its own track record. Borrowing the phrase from the Allstate Insurance commercials, you want the reader (in other words, the funder) to feel their funding is in good hands. Therefore, provide bios for you and other key players that demonstrate you and your team can provide the technical and leadership aspects the business requires.

- **There is no supporting team.** A business has lots of dimensions, areas of expertise, and moving parts. Even a single-person company can and should have advisors, contractors, and support members to make sure all key areas are covered. You started your business because you are good at marketing, creating apps, consulting, inventing new gadgets, or some other activity that generates cash flow. To have a successful company, you will also need to pay attention to accounting, distribution, customer relations, advertising, and more. Get a team to help you. Your team can take many shapes: full-time employees, part-timers, advisors, a SCORE mentor, or volunteers until funding is available to pay salaries. If any of the team has worked together before, say so.

IT'S LIKE THIS: A client developed a unique retail food concept, combining several food service venues in one. But her bio started with her law degree, awards, and publications, which are impressive but are not related to the business idea. She needed to focus her skills as they relate to the market and customer. Her bio was rewritten so it demonstrated her formidable customer and retailing experience and expertise.

Financials

- **No funding is provided by the owners.** Banks want owners with "skin in the game," which usually translates to requiring a 20 to 25 percent capital infusion by the owners, their families, and/or friends. Just like buying a house, it is rare to get a 100 percent mortgage, and likewise it is rare to receive a business loan or angel funding for the full amount needed. For some banks, not showing this owner contribution up front is reason not to proceed. Entrepreneurs requesting angel funding often have self-invested at least $50,000 to $100,000.

  In a similar fashion, investors want to know that the founder is "all in." If you maintain another position that generates a salary or other income for you and devote only part time to the start-up, it will be difficult to get funding, as the investors will feel that you have a separate safety net: If the new business has problems, you can walk away, but the investors are stuck.

- **Asking for a funding amount that is not supported by the financial statements.** In the executive summary will be a statement of how much the entrepreneur is seeking from a bank or investor. But do the financial statements back it up? It takes money to start a business, in some businesses much more than others. However, some business plan writers are so intent on demonstrating that their business idea is a big winner that the sales assumptions show it generating a large amount of cash in the first few months, which masks the funding requirement. Often entrepreneurs request larger funding than they actually need since they feel it is a negotiation and they need to ask for $100,000 to get $75,000. Yes, there is a negotiation, but the requested amount must be supported with at least a three-year cash flow projection.

IT'S LIKE THIS: The same client with the unique retail food concept said in her executive summary that she needed $190,000 to start her business and she would personally invest $40,000 and thus was looking for a $150,000 bank loan. This was a good start as it demonstrated she was investing about 20 percent of the requirements. However, 20 pages later in the cash flow statement, the lowest monthly cash ending balance was positive $125,000. The bank does not want to lend funds just to have them sit in a bank account. So either she needed much less in initial funding or her sales/expense assumptions were too optimistic.

- **Asking for funding primarily to pay your first-year salary.** In the finance section, you will list the uses of the obtained funding. Banks/angels prefer to provide money for assets or activities that will make money like buying a building or equipment, designing and building a website, funding a robust marketing program, or hiring a sales team. They understand but are more reluctant about funding your payroll. Banks generally like to see a modest starting owner's annual salary in the range of $30,000 to $35,000, which demonstrates the owner's confidence in the business prospects and the willingness to make near-term sacrifices. Some have called these start-up lean years the "mac and cheese period." Many angel funders are more flexible on owner salary and benefit levels.

IT'S LIKE THIS: A client was starting a company with funding from his state's Economic Development Agency. The state wanted to invest $2 million but insisted that the funds go for a brick-and-mortar location, not staff or equipment. He got the financing since he was able to show a set of the financials that reflected this level of investment in new construction and remodeling.

- **Not including the three basic financial statements.** Banks and angel investors want to see an income statement, cash flow statement, and balance sheet for at least a three-year forecast period, if not five, with the first year by month and subsequent years by quarter. It is preferred that these statements be prepared using the accrual rather than the cash basis of accounting. By showing both income and cash flow statements, an entrepreneur demonstrates an understanding of the difference between profits and cash flow.

- **There are no stated assumptions on which the financial statements are based.** Financial statements are charts with many numbers and few words. It is important to tell the reader the business basics. It is not a good idea to just say the assumptions are conservative, as this has become a red flag. Plus, my conservative might be different from your conservative. In front of the financial statements should be one to two pages—all text—noting the key assumptions from which the financial statements were created.

- **There is no exit strategy.** Even though the business may just be starting, it is important to have an exit strategy, especially if you are seeking angel or venture capital funding. This strategy does not have to be specific, but it should provide a concept of how it might occur—for example, a sale to a larger competitor. Investors typically have a three- to seven-year time horizon and want to know how they will be able to exit their investment and take their profits. The reason being, investors usually only get paid when they cash out. Obviously, a banker's exit is when the loan is repaid in full.

Key Lessons

✓ Committing these common mistakes will most likely have your business plan rejected by a potential bank lender or angel investor.

✓ Your plan needs to be well thought out and laid out with clear messages on why you are the right person at the right time to make this a successful business, along with the appropriate supporting information.

If you have already started writing your plan, are there any changes you will be making now that you know what the common mistakes are?

1.

2.

3.

4.

Chapter 5

FORGET ME NOT

*Smart Things to Do
When Writing Your Plan*

Now that you know what mistakes to avoid, here are some smart things you should do when writing your business plan. They cover both the content and process used to write the business plan.

Business Plan Writing Process

- **Share and bounce ideas off others while working on the business plan.** Surround yourself with mentors and advisors who can help you think through your business model and approach. Find people with experience who will give you good, objective feedback and not necessarily tell you what you want to hear. Often, family and friends are unable to fulfill this role. Seek advice from other businesses in your and other markets. Be a good listener—learn from others' mistakes and accomplishments.

IT'S LIKE THIS: A client who worked at a major telecommunications company in strategic planning wanted to start a gourmet chocolate store where customers could sample chocolates with coffee in a comfortable café environment.

She knew of only two other stores that had a similar business model: one in New York City and one in Chicago, each 500 miles from where she lived. After developing her business model, setting target pricing, and getting detailed estimates of all her costs (start-up and operating), she and her husband traveled to both cities to visit the stores. She went in and spent an hour or more with the owners (who were willing to talk to her because she was not a potential competitor), and her husband stood just outside the store noting how many paying customers they had in that period and how much they purchased. When she returned home, she plugged everything she learned, plus all the data, into her business model and financial projections. Ultimately, she decided not to start the business, because she could not find a scenario that would generate a profit.

- **Write the plan over a period of time.** Do not try to write the plan in one sitting. Write the business plan in sections, put the work aside, think about it, talk with others, do research, come back and rewrite. It takes a while to fully develop a business idea. This approach will take longer, but the plan quality will significantly improve as you learn about the business and markets.

- **Use good graphics.** Learn to use Word, Excel, PowerPoint, and other similar products, and use good formatting techniques or have someone help you with the graphics. If the plan is just for you, graphics are not necessary.

Focus

- **Start small and grow.** If possible, self-fund your start-up and then go for funding when you can create a growth-story message rather than a start-up story. Start-up statistics are grim—half of all new small businesses fail in the first five years, and the number is larger for restaurants. If this happens to you, you will be better off if you have not borrowed funds.

- **Focus on the customer, and fully understand the market.** Research the demographics and psychographics of your customer base, your ideal customer, and customer buying habits. Watch competitors, and talk with similar businesses. Browse your competitors' websites, and understand what their customers are saying about them on various social media sites.

  There are many examples of companies that don't have the best product or service, yet are very successful because they have mastered marketing and sales—giving customers what they think they need.

- **Understand your own strengths, skills, and time available.** Often start-ups consist of one employee—you, the founder. What are your skills and interests? How much time do you have available? These are important questions to calibrate your expectations and determine where and when you will need support. Know when you need to engage an accountant, lawyer, insurance agent, marketing specialist, web page designer, or other professional. This will start your management process as a business owner.

Content

- **Ensure information consistency.** All money references in the executive summary, revenue and cost assumptions, staffing levels, and financial statements need to be in sync. Likewise ensure the marketing plan is in sync with the sales forecast, and use consistent language and terminology.

- **Develop a powerful and readable message.** This is the most important item. Your business plan needs to answer the following questions: What problem are you solving that customers are willing to pay for the solution? How are your products and services unique? And why will your business idea be operationally and financially successful? This messaging should be used consistently in all collateral materials.

  Business plans contain many details. Information today comes in easily digestible bites (think online news, Twitter, instant messaging), so readers are looking for brief, attention-grabbing messages. This used to be called the "elevator pitch."

Other

- **Understand there are no entitlements and you must work hard for all achievements.** Even if you qualify for a government set-aside contract, you must still market and sell quality products and services; your business plan needs to reflect this effort.

Key Lessons

- ✓ A well-thought-out business plan occurs over time, including much interaction with others to learn the business and the market.

- ✓ If possible, start your business within the limits of your own financial resources, test the business idea, gain market traction, and then raise funds to scale up.

- ✓ Focus on the customer and the market, and develop powerful messages that demonstrate your value proposition and competitive differentiation.

- ✓ A well-presented business plan will facilitate reaching potential customers and funders.

Which of the smart tactics noted in this chapter will you use to modify your plan?

Chapter 6

FIRST STEPS

Starting with a Business Plan or Feasibility Plan

We've discussed why a business plan is written, who it is written for, various plan styles, and where to go for help and best practices. So now it is time to write your business plan, but how do you start? Figuratively you have blank pages in front of you—in reality, you have been thinking of your business idea for some time and you probably have a template on your computer waiting to be filled out.

There are two general approaches. If you are familiar with the business, have been working in the industry, and have been thinking of starting on your own for some time, it might be possible to jump to the next section of this book and write each business plan chapter. Even so, a quick feasibility and viability check might be a useful first step.

Preparing a business plan is a time-consuming and daunting task. You will never know if you get it "right" until you share it with others for funding, contracting, employment, and so on, or you begin following it as you start or grow your business. Couple this with the fact that as a small business owner, you will be working 60 to 100 hours a week and investing your personal capital. In both instances, it would be beneficial to know in advance if your business idea has a chance to be feasible and viable. So use the feasibility plan concept as a go/no-go decision for each successive stage of business planning intensity and thoroughness.

Preliminary Feasibility Plan

To get started business planning, begin small and informally. In about five pages and over a few days, describe each of the following in their own paragraph: the business idea, the value proposition, your competitive advantage, your ideal customer demographics, a few marketing ideas to attract and retain customers, a simplified sales forecast, and ideas on how the business would operate. Summarize all these thoughts with a simplified cash flow statement—annual numbers for three years. Do the results meet your needs and expectations? If you change a key assumption, does it have a major impact on cash flow?

If you generally like the results of this quick, preliminary feasibility plan, now would be a good time to visit with a SCORE, SBDC, or Women's Business Center mentor (as noted in Chapter 3) to talk through your business idea. The result of this preliminary feasibility plan and mentor discussions is a go or no-go decision. Does the business idea have feasibility and viability, does it meet your financial expectations, and is there a manageable amount of risk involved? If the answer to these questions is yes, then prepare a full feasibility plan.

Feasibility Plan

After discussions and more thought, conduct some preliminary research and get some facts about potential market size and your competitive advantages, fine-tune your business idea and your market differentiators, identify additional actions for your marketing plan, include more assumptions for your sales forecast, and make assumptions regarding staffing and sourcing of any needed supplies, location, use of the internet, and so forth. Now develop the cash flow statement—are the financial results still meeting your needs and expectations? This approach might result in five to eight pages of information and take you two weeks or less, depending on your effort level.

SCORE conducts a workshop titled "Simple Steps for Starting Your Business." This is a five-step process for developing a feasibility plan. The major themes of this workshop are start-up basics, business concept, marketing plan, financial projections, and funding.

If your feasibility plan convinces you that your business idea is feasible and viable and you can manage the risks, then you are in a go position and can continue to develop your business idea in a business plan. If your feasibility plan convinces you that there are major cracks in the business idea, then before proceeding with the business plan, keep developing the business concept, work some in the industry to understand it better and establish contacts, find additional mentors and maybe a partner, and after gaining more experience and knowledge, revisit the idea of developing a business plan and starting the business.

Key Lesson

✓ You can develop a business plan right off the bat, or you can build up to it, starting with a preliminary feasibility plan and then a full feasibility plan to check if your business idea is sound and viable.

What approach will you follow in drafting your business plan? Preliminary feasibility plan, feasibility plan, or skip feasibility planning and start with the full business plan? Why have you selected this approach?

BUSINESS PLAN CONTENTS

In this section, we will review the business plan elements in detail. The book chapters are organized like a standard business plan, and each covers the traditional content for that particular element. You, as the business plan author, can put it together in a way that you think best describes your business and provides the most critical information for your various audiences.

Spend some time thinking about your audience and what they need. If you have questions, ask them. For example, to your banker, "I am developing an idea for growing my business. I know the traditional 30-page business plan template, but what specific information do you need to review my proposal and grant a loan in the range of $75,000 to $125,000?" Or Fred might say to his small business loan officer, "I plan to start a B&B in a town 100 miles away. Is this something the bank would be interested in funding? If so, what information should I include in my business plan, which I am working with a SCORE mentor to prepare?"

At the beginning of each of the following chapters, there is short section called "Think About It." This is intended as a quick index of subjects addressed, but more important, you should use it to consider this element of your business plan in some depth. Just reading this book as a novel is not sufficient; you need to be fully engaged to get the best business plan results.

I have given catchy titles to the chapters to get your attention and give some context to what is included. However, when you write your plan, you should use the standard titles for the plan elements: Executive Summary, General Company Description, Products and Services, Marketing, Operations, Management Team and Organization, Financials, and Appendix (if needed).

Chapter 7

IN A NUTSHELL

*Why the Executive Summary Is the
Most Important Part of Your Plan*

Think About It

Does my executive summary...

- ✓ Summarize the full plan, and is it consistent with all the information that follows?

- ✓ Clearly and concisely present my business idea so a reader can fully understand it and its potential?

- ✓ Have an upbeat and enthusiastic tone as if I am on stage promoting my elevator pitch?

This is one of the shortest sections of a business plan but the one you will spend the most time working on. Whether your business plan is five or 30 pages, an executive summary must recap all the material that follows in only two pages. The reason this section gets so much attention is that it might be the only pages the reader looks at when making a decision to go forward or stop. Paraphrasing the old proverb, you can tell the quality of a business plan from its executive summary.

The executive summary is where you demonstrate the honed messages you have been working on. It is the ultimate "elevator pitch" where you introduce the idea, provide background, talk about approach and results, and convey confidence that you will be successful. Bankers and angel investors receive many funding request proposals and have limited time, so they first need to be sold on your story and its potential; then once they are excited, they will explore it further.

IT'S LIKE THIS: A client provided a draft business plan to start a sandwich shop. It was presented in a three-ring binder, with each page wrapped in a plastic jacket. The plan included a table of contents with all the appropriate elements, though each section was just a few sentences. More important, the executive summary only contained the business license, articles of incorporation, and menu. Nowhere was there a discussion to describe the market and how the restaurant would be successful. This entrepreneur focused on the details long before making the case that this was a worthy business idea and she was the right person to lead the effort. The details she provided belonged in the sections that followed, not in the executive summary.

Topics Covered

At the very beginning of the executive summary, describe your business and the customer problem being uniquely solved so that in one paragraph, the reader understands what you are trying to achieve.

In the marketing paragraphs, note the size of the market, sales forecast, demographics of your potential customers and competition, and your competitive advantages. Also, provide enough description of your plans to identify, attract, and retain customers that it convinces the reader the sales forecast is reasonable.

In the operations/staffing/management paragraphs, demonstrate management's leadership and industry experience, along with a few key details about the location, staffing, and operations.

The financial paragraphs should include a clear statement of how much is needed to start the business, and of this sum, how much you will be investing versus the amount being sought from the funder. Also, include the projected income earned and cash generated during the first three years and how the new funds will be used.

Charts or Text Only?

A question many entrepreneurs ask is, should the executive summary be all text or should there be some charts to "liven it up"? The general answer is yes. Charts and graphs do make it more interesting, but it is often hard to cram all that needs to be said into two pages. So here is the first instance of knowing your audience and what style they like. If it is not possible to include both text and charts, then include more text and fewer pictures. When you use a chart, make sure it tells a believable and compelling message. The most commonly used charts show the growth of revenues, profits, and/or customers.

And remember that while the executive summary appears first in the business plan, it should be written last since it is the summary. A business plan is developed from the bottom up, so you need to work out all the details before you can write the summary.

Key Lessons

✓ First impressions are important, so the executive summary should have an enthusiastic tone and be concise, professional, and complete.

✓ In two pages, it should be a summary of everything that follows— all key messages and issues should be addressed.

Have you tried to write the executive summary first, to get an idea of how the plan will look and feel? That's a natural tendency, but spend the time working on the other sections first and then come back to it. When you return, write one or two sentences on the following worksheet that summarize the key points from each of the other sections. This will form the backbone content of your executive summary.

General Company Description	
Products and Services	
Marketing	
Operations	
Management Team and Organization	
Financials	

Chapter 8

GET ORGANIZED

Presenting Your General Company Description

Think About It

Does my general company description...

✓ Describe my company's legal structure, ownership, and contact information?

✓ Include my company mission statement?

✓ Include key goals?

The general company description section is usually just one page; sometimes one paragraph is sufficient. The key information to include is a description of what business you are in, your mission statement and key goals, the legal form of organization (for example, sole proprietorship, LLC, S corp, C corp, partnership), in which state the organization was formed, contact information, and a listing of the owners with their shares. If you have not applied to become a certain type of organization, then you are a sole proprietorship—the default option. A nonprofit is formed as a corporation in a particular state and then applies to the IRS and state for nonprofit status, which may be received six months later (see Chapter 15 for more nonprofit specifics).

Note: For companies with more than one owner, you should document, probably in the operating agreement (for LLC or partnerships) or shareholder agreement (for C and S corps) and not in the business plan, how decisions get made, how existing owners can sell their shares and new owners join, and how to allocate profits and losses among the owners.

TYPES OF LEGAL STRUCTURES

While not an exhaustive discussion on the various legal forms of organization, the following is a summary of the key provisions and implications for a small business:

Sole Proprietorship

This is the only organizational form where you do not have to apply and ask permission to adopt this type of operation. For that reason, it can be considered the default organizational form. You wake up one morning, decide to be in business, and you are a sole proprietor. Of course, you may still need to register your business with the state and/or county, obtain a business license depending on the nature of the business, and prepare other paperwork to start your business.

As the term "sole" implies, this is an organization with one owner. So a husband and wife cannot be a sole proprietorship. This relates to ownership and not the number of employees. A wife could be the sole owner and employ her husband and many other employees or vice versa.

As there is no personal liability protection in a sole proprietorship, an adverse action by your business can impact your personal affairs (in other words, a legal suit can end in a claim against your personal assets). While this may sound dire, for many small businesses, there may be few instances when this may occur.

When filing taxes for your sole proprietorship, use your personal IRS Schedule 1040 and attach Schedule C ("Profit or Loss from Business"), which, in effect, is a mini business income statement. Therefore, you should account for your business as a separate entity from your personal affairs. On Schedule C, owner's compensation is not an expense line item because it assumes that the difference between revenues and expenses, meaning net income, is equal to the owner's salary. It is on this amount that you will be assessed payroll taxes, via Form SE ("Self-Employment Taxes"), and on this amount, you can create a Simplified Employee Pension Individual Retirement Account (SEP-IRA) and reduce your taxable income.

Limited Liability Company (LLC)

This organizational form has the personal liability protection benefits of a corporation without having all the required administrative and governance procedures. To obtain LLC status, you must apply to a state by submitting an application with an annual fee (each state is different, but it is generally in the $100 to $200 range).

With the state-approved LLC, there will be an operating agreement—think company bylaws. These will be the general rules for your company governance. In most cases, the state's standard operating agreement is satisfactory, especially if you are a single-member LLC. However, if there are several founding members, you will want to review the operating agreement and make sure it fits your situation with an agreement and understanding among the co-owners. This is your operating agreement, so you can fashion it to your situation. The unique items to each group of founding members are who is empowered to make which decisions, how does a member sell his/her shares and exit the business, what are the procedures for admitting new members, and how will profits and losses be allocated among the members.

Entrepreneurs frequently select the LLC format to obtain personal assets liability protection. Many start-ups and most "idea" businesses have few assets, so a suit against the company will have no reward and the claimant will try to go after personal assets. But just because you have the LLC paperwork, this will not automatically provide the desired liability protection if you do not operate the LLC as a separate entity. So keep all parts of your business separate from your personal affairs—have a separate bank account, credit/debit card, letterhead business stationery, and so forth.

Where it becomes more difficult in keeping this separation is in obtaining funding. As will be discussed later, with a start-up or a business with few assets, the funder will demand assurances and collateral. This usually translates to a personal guarantee and a lien on your personal assets. Some lawyers might argue this is sufficient to say that the LLC is not a separate entity and personal and business interests have been joined. Part of this separation of personal and business activities is to be alert to the fact that you most likely will have two roles and wear two hats: one as LLC employee and one as LLC owner.

As an LLC owner, there are options on how to be taxed for federal and state income tax purposes. Most entrepreneurs select to have the LLC be considered as a tax pass-through entity and pay the taxes on their personal return(s), since, for most, the personal tax rate is lower than the corporate tax rate. So the LLC will file an information tax return to the IRS (no money is sent) and the owner(s) report and pay their agreed share on their personal tax returns.

Subchapter S Corporation

This form of organization has characteristics of both the LLC and C corp. There can be no more than 100 shareholders who are U.S. citizens or residents. Application is made to a state along with an annual filing fee.

The subchapter S corporation will have a shareholders' agreement. These are your bylaws, so design them to meet your needs. You will have a board of directors and the corporate governance processes that apply. As this is a corporation, you can use "Inc." in your company name, which to some is important, but to me is overrated. In some states, for example, California and Texas, if you are a subchapter S corporation or a C corporation, you must use "Inc." in your name or otherwise disclose your corporation status so potential customers and vendors know claims against the company will be subject to corporate vs. sole proprietor asset safeguards.

Like the LLC, in an S corp, there are elections to be made on taxation, and most entrepreneurs select to report and pay the federal and state income tax on their personal tax return.

C Corporation

C corporation is the legal form of organization adopted by most publicly traded companies. A C corp is a separate legal entity, a "person" under the law. Of all the organizational forms, this one has the most administrative and governance requirements, including a board of directors who have the ultimate fiduciary responsibility.

Since the C corp is a separate "person," it pays corporate income tax. When distributions are made to the owners via dividends, these are taxed to the recipients. The term "double taxation" is used to describe this process.

IT'S LIKE THIS: A client prepares a draft business plan and has already applied for, paid for, and received approval to be a C corp. When asked why he chose this organizational form, the response is that including "Inc." in the business name is important as it gives some gravitas to a small start-up organization. If this is important, then OK, but know all the administrative and governance requirements you must comply with each year. You can also use "Inc." if your company is set up as a subchapter S, which comes with much fewer administrative headaches. Most customers do not know or care about the suffix in a company name but do care about its products, services, and reputation.

Nonprofit

To become a nonprofit, first apply to a state to be a corporation under its Nonprofit Corporation Act, and then apply to the IRS on Form 1023 for 501(c)(3) or another of the nonprofit designations, and finally back to the state for its certification. (This is discussed more fully in Chapter 15.) While 501(c)(3) is the most common nonprofit form, under the IRC code in section 501, there are about 25 different nonprofit designations, depending on the type of activities/services provided.

Benefit Corporation

This structure is new (Maryland was the first state to permit it in 2010), and as of 2015, it is authorized in 31 states with seven more considering it. This structure includes the positive impact on society, workers, community, and environment, in addition to profit, as legally defined company goals. Benefit corporations differ from S and C corps in purpose, accountability, and transparency but not taxation. It is focused on for-profit entities that have a specific social mission. Boards of directors must consider not only the financial implications of their decisions but also the social and environmental impact. Without this structure, boards who consider social and environmental impacts to the detriment of financial factors might be sued for not properly representing shareholders. With this structure, boards can be sued for not considering these nonfinancial items. Some entrepreneurs like this organization form as they feel it more accurately represents their dual social and profit purposes. Among the states, there is some competition as they would like more companies with this designation to be registered in their state. A variation of this approach is the Low-Profit Limited Liability Company (L3C). Keep in mind, this is all new and untested.

Make sure you understand the organizational implications of each organization form; if you are unsure, seek professional assistance. For example, with all but sole proprietorships and LLCs, you must have a board of directors since the rest are a type of corporation. With an LLC, you can choose to have a board, but it is not a requirement.

For all organization types, you can, and I encourage you to, have a board of advisors. See Chapter 33, "Advice on Tap," for an in-depth discussion on formal and advisory boards.

Your selection of a business organization form does not have to be a forever decision. You can start with a sole proprietorship or LLC, and when business needs change, convert to an S or C corp.

IT'S LIKE THIS: A client was planning on licensing her artwork to be used on fabrics, porcelain, and other items for retail sales. She was planning to use most of the profits to support a charity she is very close to. She considered forming a benefit corporation since she would be permitted to consider items other than profit in making decisions. She started her market research for donors/investors who would help get the business started. Launching any business is difficult, but starting one with a structure few have heard of confused her messaging (too much time on organization and not enough on her mission). She decided to form a nonprofit instead.

IT'S LIKE THIS: A musically oriented group had been donating their time to their church and performing at children's groups to preach their faith. They decided it was time to get paid for their services, so they formed a C corp and applied for nonprofit status. When asked for a list of their board members, they said the owners were the only members. They did not understand that in many states, paid employees cannot be on their own nonprofit board and they would have to find other people to operate under this structure. Even if the state allowed this, it is not a best governance practice.

The following table is provided since many clients ask for a comparison of S corps and LLCs, which both provide liability protection to the LLC members and S corp shareholders.

ATTRIBUTES	S CORP	LLC
Number of Shareholders/Owners	No more than 100	Unlimited
Owner's Nationality	Only U.S.	Anyone
Types of Owners	Individuals	Individuals, other LLCs, corporations, foreign entities
Issuing Stock for Additional Funding	Yes	No
Transferability of Ownership	Each owner can freely sell their interest (stock) in the company.	Each member may have to gain approval of other members to sell and may be limited on who they can sell to.
Tax Pass-Through Election—Profits and Losses Tax on Owner's/Member's Personal Tax Return	Yes	Yes
Formula for Distribution of Profits and Losses	Strictly in proportion to ownership interest	Flexible to set by agreement and noted in the operating agreement
Governance Formality	Requirements for a board of directors, bylaws, board and annual meetings, board and board committee minutes, etc.	Most states require an operating agreement; all else is by choice.
Self-Employment Taxes	Distributions only subject to these taxes up to the amount of "reasonable income"	All distributions are subject to self-employment taxes *(however, you can elect to be taxed as an S corp or partnership to eliminate some self-employment taxes)*.
Annual Tax Information Return to the IRS	Yes, Form 1120S	Yes, most LLCs with more than one member file a partnership return, Form 1065. If you file as a corporation, then use Form 8832. Generally, when an LLC has one member, LLC status is "disregarded" for the purpose of filing a federal tax return. However, operationally/legally the business remains an LLC.

MISSION AND GOALS

Your mission statement outlines the purpose of your organization and will guide your decisions and actions, so you need to share it with those you are planning to do business with, be they external funders or internal employees. Your mission statement is an expression of purpose and direction and does not contain confidential information.

When you start a business, you will have more "to dos" than time permits. You need to figure out what is crucial to accomplish to implement your business idea. Sharing these goals will facilitate getting others to help you.

Key Lessons

✓ A sole proprietorship is the default form of company organization. You do not need to apply to become a sole proprietorship, but you may still need to register your business. With all other company forms, there is a state application and annual fee.

✓ To become a nonprofit is a three-step application process—state, IRS, state.

✓ Understand the governance and reporting requirements of the organization form you select, as it can have an impact on the way you organize and your costs.

✓ Selecting a business organization form does not have to be forever. You can start with a sole proprietorship or LLC and at some future time change to an S or C corp.

List your mission statement.

List your three to five key goals covering the next 12 months.

1.

2.

3.

4.

5.

What is your legal form of organization, state in which it was formed, and principal place of business address, telephone number, fax number, email address, and website URL (if you have one)?

List the owners by name with their ownership interest (for many, this will be just you at 100 percent).

Chapter 9

LIKE NO OTHER

Describing Your Products and Services

Think About It

Does my products and services description...

✓ Fully and clearly define my products and services?

✓ Make my competitive advantage clear?

✓ Describe "protections" for my competitive advantage?

✓ Describe the customer need that is being uniquely satisfied from the purchase of my product or service?

In this section, you provide a full description of your products and services. While referenced here, technical specifications, drawings, photos, and sales brochures belong in an appendix or should be available on request since they are often bulky. Mention your channels of distribution (for example, retail, wholesale, consignment, internet), and also include any intellectual property (IP) "protections" you have or plan to apply for, like patents, trademarks, or copyrights. Understanding the durability and scope of your IP protections is important to angel and venture capital funders as they want to ensure the projected cash flows are secure.

The benefit of having a patent is it protects your good idea from competitors and thus helps secure your profits and cash flow—important to you and potential funders. However, patents are not free—it takes many months to research existing patents, prepare and file your application, and engage a patent attorney. I have seen estimates of $10,000 to over $100,000 to file with the U.S. Patent and Trademark Office. And depending on the business and your markets, you might need to file in other jurisdictions as well.

However, just because you may have a patent, doesn't mean a competitor won't copy it. Of course, you can send cease-and-desist letters, but eventually you may have to go to court, and this could be very expensive. Small businesses usually do not have the necessary financial resources, but if you have a strong patent and a good patent attorney, maybe they will take the case on a contingency basis.

What's Your Competitive Advantage?

What factors give you competitive advantages or disadvantages? Your product or service should be unique in some way; otherwise, customers may go to your competitors. These factors may include level of quality or service, proprietary features that have IP protections, location, and hours of operation.

Note that lowest price is not mentioned for two reasons. First, if this is your sole competitive advantage, it will be very easy for a competitor to undercut you. Second, and more important, in our materialistic culture, there is a clear consumer perception that you get what you pay for, so if your product/service is the cheapest, maybe something is wrong with it. This buying preference is demonstrated over and over in marketing studies; even people at a restaurant who are buying a bottle of wine but watching their budget will most likely purchase the second-cheapest bottle.

If you are describing a service, your competitive advantage may be that you are local. Since it is often the entrepreneur who personally performs the service and you are marketing to a small local market rather than a national one, your business description and marketing information should clearly indicate that is what makes your service stand apart.

It is natural to describe products and services as they physically appear—for example, a machine replacement part, a food item, a report, an hour of yoga instruction, and so on. But you should also describe your product and/or service from the customer's perspective, including what customer needs are being fulfilled from the purchase of your product or service as well as the benefit the customer receives from the purchase. For example, using the four items above, you might say reducing plant downtime, satisfying a hunger, information on which to make a business decision, and good health.

Product Development Roadmap

When you first consider starting your business, you have a product/ service idea—a machine, a machine part, an app, enterprise software, a retail product, etc. As you progress, the idea turns into a prototype, then a minimum viable product, then a version 1, version 2, and so on. Several years after start-up, you might be on version 4.3. You should explain the product development sequence in a time line and cost chart, called a product development roadmap.

A product development roadmap pictorially shows how your product will be developed and enhanced over time. The key information to include is what are the additions and their timing, who is involved, and what is the cost. With this analysis, you can plan your marketing and sales efforts and go-to-market strategy. A search online for "product development roadmap template" yields hundreds of examples. The "Multiple Product Roadmap" shown here is just one example.

Multiple Project Roadmap

2016	Q3			Q4		
Jun	Jul	Aug	Sep	Oct	Nov ▾	Dec

˅ Product 1
- › Web Platform
- › Web Platform 2.0
- Distribution

˅ Product 2
- › Mobile Platform
- Mobile Monitoring Solution
- › Marketing Campaign

˅ Product 3
- › Localized CRM
- › Cloud Support
- Market Problems
- Market Opportunities
- › Data Logging Module

Status: ▧ In Development ■ Approved ▨ Planned ■ Completed

This roadmap will be good input for developing the financial information in Chapter 13, "Number Sense." It will help you explain to investors what you need their money for, negotiate with developers/manufacturers, and link your product and marketing strategies. The products and services section also contains an industry overview, including trends, major players, and estimated industry sales.

Key Lessons

✓ Having some protections like patents and copyrights make your products and services more valuable and harder for competitors to copy.

✓ To be successful means you are profitably taking business away from the competition. To achieve this, you must have some unique feature that makes purchasing from you attractive.

✓ In addition to describing the physical attributes of your product or service, note the customer problem being solved or need satisfied.

List your products and services, their unique features, and how your customers see these as satisfying a need.

PRODUCT/SERVICE	UNIQUE FEATURES	CUSTOMER NEED SATISFIED

For each product or service, list the intellectual property protection you have or plan to have.

PRODUCT/SERVICE	IP (PATENT, TRADEMARK, TRADE SECRET)

Chapter 10

GOING TO MARKET

Writing Your Marketing Plan

Think About It

Does my marketing plan...

✓ Describe my potential customers?

✓ Have an analysis of my competition, my niche, and likely competitor reaction?

✓ Demonstrate that my marketing is targeted to my potential customers?

✓ Describe the marketing actions I will take, including time and cost involved?

✓ Conclude with a "believable" sales forecast and marketing budget?

For many entrepreneurs, this is the most important section and much time is devoted to developing it. For without demand, there are no sales and there is nothing to account for. A marketing plan has three principal sections: 1) market analysis, 2) competitive analysis, and 3) specific marketing actions. Of all the business plan elements, the marketing section requires the most continual updates. Marketing campaigns come and go, and as your business needs change, the "tools" to implement your marketing campaign will change as well.

MARKET ANALYSIS

The purpose of this section is twofold. First is figuring out how big the market is; you need to know if there will be sufficient customers to buy your product or service so you can generate satisfactory revenue. The second purpose is to describe your potential or ideal customer so you will know how to reach that market when conducting your outreach.

Can you visualize your target market—a group of potential customers who share certain characteristics, needs, or interests? Do your customers share a common age range, income level, gender, residence area, type of work, religion, family structure, hobbies, diet, ethnicity, etc.? If you have a business-to-business (B2B) company, do your potential customers have a certain size in terms of sales or staffing, order size and frequency, payment practices, contracting formalities, etc.?

IT'S LIKE THIS: A few years ago, I sold a house. I asked several real estate reps to write a proposal to be my agent; all came with marketing plans that included the typical newspaper ads and open houses. Within the proposal, I asked each realtor to describe the likely family to buy the house. One agent said a professional couple with two to three children enrolled in the neighborhood schools, who are looking to "move up" without changing school districts. This agent won my business, marketed to this type of customer—and ended up describing the exact family who bought my house.

IT'S LIKE THIS: A client planned to provide systems and billing functions for small medical group practices. It was a good niche market, but there was a lack of homework on how doctors make decisions on such support and if they even wanted to outsource these efforts. The plan failed to convince banks to make a loan to buy the software.

With today's powerful internet search engines, there is no shortage of information to aid in your market research. You will be surprised how much information can be obtained with little effort.

Here are a number of sources to check out:

- **Census Bureau (www.census.gov):** On this site (and some of its specialty sites like Fact Finder at http://factfinder2.census.gov and Quick Facts at http://quickfacts.census.gov), you can get information about population counts by age, gender, and race, and income level by street and block location. Of course, you will need to know your business and what is important. For example, if you are starting an internet business that is dependent on viewer subscriptions and advertising revenues, you do not care about information to the block level. However, if you are opening a coffee shop and know that customers usually buy coffee within a three-mile radius of home or within two city blocks of a downtown office, then detailed block level information is very important.

- **Library of Congress "Ask a Librarian" Service (www.loc.gov/ rr/askalib):** This is an excellent free reference resource where you can ask to see specific books or get your questions answered about a variety of business topics, such as foreign exchange rates (which might be helpful if you are importing or exporting) or the history of a company (which might be useful if you are planning to do business with another company).

- **Trade Associations:** There is a trade association, professional society, collectors club, and more for just about every topic, and most have newsletters and information about their membership. Do an internet search to find the websites for associations in your industry where you can learn about licensing requirements and number of firms (i.e., competitors) in an area. Some may also have information about how to start a business in their field, a contact you can speak with who might share what it is like to be in this particular business, and more.

- **D&B (www.dnb.com) and Hoovers (www.hoovers.com):** Use D&B and its subsidiary Hoovers to create potential customer lists with good contact information. You can also sign up for their subscription service to research a customer's history and company reports, and learn how they pay their bills.

Sometimes the best information is gained from a little in-person research:

- **Competitors:** Go visit a few competitors as a potential customer, and take note of how many customers are in the store, whether they are browsing or buying, how the store is laid out, what the quality of the merchandise and the pricing is, and all the other aspects you think about when setting up your business. Also, travel to another city where you will not be considered a competitor and observe the same items mentioned above for local competitors, but also, hopefully, discuss with the owner their lessons learned. If you are new to the industry, work for an established firm for a while to gain industry knowledge. These firsthand views are not meant to "copy" competitors but to use real-world examples to shape your own goals and methods. Do not forget they *are* competitors. Antitrust laws dictate what can and cannot be shared between competitors. See Chapter 32,

"Walking the Line," for the basic do's and don'ts of competitor interactions.

- **Libraries:** Many libraries have a business section where you can find books on your industry. Many also subscribe to ReferenceUSA (www.referenceusa.com), which bills itself as the premier source of businesses and consumer information for reference and research. At some libraries, this source can only be used on-site while others allow remote access with a valid username and password.

The result of these investigations and research should be a full description of your potential market—its size and demographics so you know if enough revenue can be generated and so you can visualize your customer and know how to reach them.

You should differentiate between the markets you are going after: the total market and the total addressable market (TAM). Here is an example of the difference: Your total market is education, a very large market. But your TAM might be more narrowly described as in-home tutoring, or even more precise, in-home tutoring K-12 or in-home tutoring SAT preparation.

As you do this market research on the TAM, keep in mind that several types of businesses can have multiple sets of customers. For example, a nonprofit has clients it serves and donors it solicits for fundraising. A staffing business has business customers that need temporary help and individuals who are looking to do temporary work.

This review and analysis can be two pages or less.

IT'S LIKE THIS: In the Washington, DC, metro area, many entrepreneurs want to sell to the government and think just by stating this that they have focused on the customer. In the area, there are about 320,000 civilian government employees (in other words, nonmilitary and non-postal service), and in total, there may be as many as 1,300 distinct government organizations across the three branches of federal government. It is wise to focus on just two or three agencies so you can really understand what they are about and what their needs are, and figure out how you can help them solve their problems. An excellent book for learning how to sell to the federal government is *Government Contracts Made Easier*, by Judy Bradt.

IT'S LIKE THIS: A client wanted to open a coffee shop to cater to an ethnic group. He wanted to copy the Starbucks concept of providing reading space and expand it to have games. While the concept had merits, market research showed the targeted community was not large enough to make the venture economically viable—there would probably not be sufficient customers to more than offset the costs involved. This is exactly why research is so important; you do not want to start a commitment that has a low chance of success. The client is now exploring other opportunities.

COMPETITIVE ANALYSIS

A familiar refrain from start-up entrepreneurs is that they believe their business is unique and they have no competition. Sorry, but every business has competition. After all, all customers who might want your product or service today bought it or something like it from a competitor yesterday. Your goal is to find out who those competitors are so you can take the business from them.

The point of this section of your business plan is to list about five competitors and their strengths and weaknesses. In some cases, especially with brick-and-mortar businesses, a map of competitor locations is helpful to include in the plan, especially if you are approaching banks for funds and want to demonstrate how far away direct competitors are.

Listing the strengths and weaknesses of your competitors is important as it will provide insight for the next section of the marketing plan. Typically, strengths and weaknesses include operating hours, accessibility, pricing, return policy, marketing budget size, reputation, delivery policy (is it provided free, at cost, or not at all?), complementary products and services, current/outdated versions (which might also apply to current/outdated styles), and buying quantities (which may equate to lower or higher costs).

As part of your competitive analysis, it is important to understand what a competitor's reactions might be to you as a new market entrant. For example, competitors might lower their prices, copy your products, increase their advertising budget, use attack ads, provide free delivery or other services, and more. These actions might impact your sales and/or your margins and should be reflected in your sales and financial forecasts. Some entrepreneurs find it useful to summarize this competitive analysis in a "SWOT matrix," where SWOT stands for a competitor's strengths, weaknesses, opportunities, and threats. You might also conduct this SWOT analysis on your own company to understand how a competitor might view you.

IT'S LIKE THIS: A client produced T-shirts with religious pictures and quotations. She planned to sell them at a local flea market on weekends. The client did not think through what sellers of similar items would do in reaction to her potentially taking business away from them. She found that competitors quickly created their own supply of similar T-shirts, so her actual sales were only one-third of what she had forecast.

Another Way to Look at Your Competition

The above competitive analysis discussion focused on finding out "who" your competition is. You might think of this as the supply side—others providing the same or a similar product or service. For example, if you are planning to open a coffee shop, you need to determine where the other coffee shops are or, if you are planning a market research consulting practice, who else provides such a service—you are probably all members of the same professional organization.

A more interesting and insightful way of thinking about your competition is to consider the "what," which is the demand side. What is the potential customer looking for? The customer might be thirsty and within one-quarter mile has options for two coffee shops, a convenience store, a vending machine at a gas station, a public water fountain, and more. Another customer might need transportation of raw materials to his plant and will be thinking not only of competitor trucking firms close to yours but also rail and plane alternatives. So when thinking about the competition, think broadly.

MARKETING ACTION PLAN APPROACH

The goal of this section is to develop marketing-related action items to implement your business idea. In other words, what are you going to do to drive traffic to your front door—both literally and figuratively? From the list of typical marketing action steps starting on page 100 as well as your own ideas, what are the five marketing steps you will be undertaking? For each of the five marketing steps, note the cost to implement (which, when totaled, becomes your marketing budget), if the items can be completed by you alone or whether you will need assistance, and the sales expectations (which, when added together, become the sales forecast). The marketing budget and sales forecast developed in this chapter will be information used in the financial forecasts discussed in Chapter 13.

Put the Marketing Action Steps in Context

As you think about which marketing actions steps to take, consider the following strategy-planning questions:

- **Where do potential customers go for information?** From your market research and analysis, you should know where your existing and potential customers go to get information and recommendations for new products and services. This research should be the foundation of your marketing action plan because this is where you want to promote your products and/or services.

- **Should the focus be on obtaining new customers or on gaining repeat business from existing customers?** Many businesses calculate that it is less expensive to keep existing customers than to develop new ones. Of course, a start-up has only one choice, but an established business has both options. In her recent book, *Engagement Marketing: How Small Business Wins in a Socially Connected World*, Gail F. Goodman, former CEO of Constant Contact, a company providing tools and resources to make marketing easy and affordable for small businesses and nonprofits, notes that for small retailers, 90 percent of sales come from repeat customers and only 10 percent from new customers. Of those new customers, 90 percent comes from word of mouth and referrals from existing customers and 10 percent from new marketing efforts. Thus, only 1 percent of small retail customers are new customers resulting from company marketing efforts, yet this is where much of the marketing budget is spent. Goodman suggests focusing on the 99 percent, which can be done using low-cost techniques.

Marketing/Sales Cycle

Before you choose which marketing action steps to take, you must understand how potential customers reach a buying decision.

There are many models of the marketing/sales cycle, sometimes called the buying or selling cycle. One that is quite useful is from Jeanne Rossomme, founder and CEO of Roadmap Marketing (www.roadmapmarketing.com), a marketing consulting firm.

Buy Cycle

The buy cycle has six steps, which end in obtaining a happy customer who makes referrals. While graphically and conceptually this is a linear process, in reality, customers and potential customers move in and out of the steps at their choosing. Following is a description of each step:

1. **Awareness:** In this first step, potential customers know that your company is open for business and you might have the products and services they are looking for, or, more directly, that you have products and services that will satisfy a customer need. They know this from your website, having heard you speak at a convention, from advertisements, through word of mouth, and more.

2. **Discovery:** In this stage, the prospective customer finds out a little more about your business, usually through content, such as your web pages, social media reviews, literature, or from others.

3. **Engagement:** The potential customer takes an action that might lead to a sale. They might visit your store, send you an email with a question, sign up for a newsletter or notices of events/sales, and so forth. The key in this stage is that the potential customer "gives" something to express interest (like an email address or their time via a visit to your store).

4. **Active Customer:** The customer has purchased your product or service.

5. **Successful Customer:** The customer makes repeat purchases and, if measured via a survey, will say they are a satisfied customer.

6. **Referrals:** In this final step, the customer tells others about the good experience they had with your company and recommends your business to others. In essence, they become your external sales team. Capture these referrals/testimonials, and get permission to publish them in your literature and on your website.

Choosing Your Action Items

Following is a list of more than 20 typical marketing action steps grouped into seven categories. As you select marketing action items, ensure you have a variety that focus on customers in each of the six steps of the buy cycle. While some of the "instruments" might be the same, the messages may be different. For example, in a direct marketing campaign to gain awareness, you want to steer potential customers to your website, but for active customers, you may offer a store coupon. Similarly, in a social media campaign, you could use the following methods for customers in various stages of the buy cycle: To promote customer awareness, provide links to your website; in the discovery phase, target customers who are followers or fans; in the engagement phase, get potential customers to "like" and comment on your Facebook page; and in the referral stage, ask customers to "retweet" your messages. As you can see, saying you will be using social media to attract customers is not sufficient. Your marketing plan must be very detailed.

Further, each of these marketing actions has a set of economics—the cost and time to produce vs. the rewards to be achieved. To make sure your time and money are well spent, you should determine in advance how you will measure the success of these actions. If you cannot measure the cost vs. gain, maybe you should not undertake the action. Most entrepreneurs have limited budgets, so prioritize your marketing dollars and only use those actions that will provide the best results.

Email Marketing

- Email marketing includes direct emails to your customer base, newsletters, surveys, and polls—all items to keep existing customers engaged. Constant Contact (www.constantcontact.com) is one company that offers a complete suite of inexpensive, easy-to-use templates and mechanisms for keeping in touch with your customers. Be sure to inform your audience of the frequency of your newsletters and other publications, make sure the content is relevant, and remind clients that they can unsubscribe at any time.

Affiliates, Distributors, and Referring Partners

Affiliates, distributors, and referring partners include other organizations that you may do business with on an ongoing or specifically contracted basis, such as trade associations, venues for selling your products, other companies you partner with, and more.

- Exhibit at expos and trade association events. There may be a cost to have a vendor table, but if it is the right audience and there is time for the meeting participants to visit the vendor area, it might be a great deal. Ask for 15 minutes of podium time to promote your business, and, in trade, sponsor a coffee table. Network and network again, capturing relevant email addresses for future contact.

- Set up a table at craft fairs, art markets, farmers markets, flea markets, and other venues. By first being a potential customer yourself, you can get a feel for these venues to see which attract your potential customers. As customers approach your table, engage them in a discussion on what they are looking for, what quality and price range they seek, what they think of this venue, and other topics. If they cannot find what they are looking for, suggest they visit your website to see your other products, and ask if they would be interested in receiving your announcements and other post-show marketing follow-up.

- Use your status as a small business, woman-owned business, minority-owned business, veteran-owned business, or disabled business owner to gain government contracts. To be a government contractor, you need to register your business with the system of award management (SAM). To register, you will need a D-U-N-S number, NAICS code, SIC code, Federal Tax ID number, etc. Go to www.SBA.gov for the full details. Before attempting this route, understand the dynamics of when you will get paid—often it is 60 days or more after submitting an invoice, with the requirement that the invoice be almost "perfect." For this marketing action step and all the others relating to government contracting, networking with agencies, prime contractors, and competitors is an important ingredient in your overall marketing plan.

- It is often difficult for a start-up to become a prime government contractor from the outset, so consider being a subcontractor to a successful prime contractor. Often this is an excellent way to launch a government contracting business. Just be sure you understand there may be tensions with the prime contractor who "controls" the relationship with the federal agency and may be reluctant to allow subcontractors access to their customer. Understand the various contracting "set asides" the government has for small businesses in general and specifically for women-, minority-, Native American-, disabled-, and veteran-owned businesses, and use this knowledge in your proposal.

- Another way for small businesses to do business with the federal government is through General Services Administration (GSA) Schedules, which are usually repetitive, non-technical procurements managed by the GSA on behalf of many government agencies. To get on a GSA schedule takes several months with a series of price negotiations. And once on the GSA schedule, a marketing effort is still required to get federal agencies to contact you for doing business, and then there will be another price negotiation.

Website

Many businesses should have a website, and it needs to be optimized for mobile access, since today more than half (according to comSource) of all visits are via smartphone or tablet. I have seen some predictions that the percentage is higher for small businesses. But before engaging a website designer, you must understand what you expect visitors to do when they reach your website. If your website is just for visibility, with mostly static information, then a low-cost generic approach provided by the likes of Godaddy.com, Wix.com, or others is probably sufficient. However, if customers need functionality to make purchases, ask questions, or do research, or you want a blog, then a customized website might be the ticket. Before hiring a website developer, get references. Then once the design is finished, verify that your website looks professional and reflects well on your company and the way you conduct business.

- List your company in a local information source. This used to be easy as there was just one answer—the Yellow Pages. Now there are many popular and inexpensive opportunities, such as Google Places (including Google reviews and Google+ Local), Yahoo Local, and Bing Local, as well as sites like Patch.com, which combine news, weather, events, chat rooms, and business directories. Yelp.com and other similar sites are like the Yellow Pages with customer reviews. Foursquare is a location-based social networking tool for mobile devices. Some local search sites cater to specific audiences like Hispanics. Also, there are the national platforms like Craigslist and Angie's List. For many of these sites, it is easier and more profitable for the vendor to gather what information they can about all businesses (even if it is incomplete or wrong), then invite businesses to "claim" their listing, at which time you can edit the information and maybe add text, pictures, videos, and other details.

Direct Mail

Direct mail is not just sales letters in business-sized envelopes; it can encompass a variety of marketing materials, including postcards, fliers, oversized postcards with pictures and graphics, brochures, newsletters, and coupon circulars—anything to capture reader interest.

Press and Media

- If your customers are newspaper readers, newspaper ads might be the way to go, but they should be considered a strategy requiring multiple occurrences—one-time ads are usually not effective in building awareness and creditability.

- Advertise in professional journals and newsletters. There is usually a cost for this, but from your research, you may have found that this is a target group you need to be in front of.

- Purchase radio and TV advertising if your customers and potential customers listen to the radio or watch television. Just make sure the ads play on the stations and at the times of day that your customers are listening and watching.

- Nonprofits should consider PSAs (public service announcements). Many TV stations have low or sometimes free rates for these ads at off-peak hours. The only cost involved is the expense of producing the ad.

- Distribute fliers and post notices in local stores, churches, and bulletin boards. Does your notice stand out, does it have the right information, and is it placed where your potential customers go for information?

- Produce a marketing brochure. Is your document of adequate design and quality to reflect well on your business and the way you do business? Customers do make assumptions based on first impressions. Once you have the brochure, how are you going to get it in front of your target customer group? These brochures can have multiple uses—for example, as a mailer or a leave-behind for face-to-face cold calls.

- Write an advice column about your industry/product/ service. Newspapers, society and trade association journals, and newsletters are always looking for good content, and since it is probably free, it is a "win win." The win for you is access to a potential customer group and over time becoming a recognized expert where customers come to you.

- Make presentations at trade association or membership groups. This is a good way to be in front of potential customers and is more active than writing in the association's newsletter. Ask for 15 minutes of podium time, and in trade, you offer to sponsor a free coffee and soda table during a break.

- If you have a physical location, you will want to have a sign to both direct customers to your front door and to inform those passing by that you are there. Location as well as visibility from many angles is important. Signage requirements are usually dictated by local zoning and building codes and, if in shopping centers or other leased locations, by landlord-tenant agreements.

- Write a book. It takes a while and can be expensive, but this is a great opportunity to develop your credentials as an expert.

Social Media

Use social media in its many dimensions. Just realize it is a tool, a means to get desired results; it is not the end. According to Brian Moran of Brian Moran & Associates, a consulting firm that helps entrepreneurs run better companies and assists marketers in reaching small businesses, you should use social media for lead generation, customer service, market research, competitor analysis, networking, and PR—and little by little, you will become the recognized expert. By knowing your customers, you can determine which of the social media is best suited for your business. As with all the other tactics we have discussed, go where your potential customers are. Each of the popular social media venues—Facebook, Twitter, LinkedIn, and Pinterest—has its own demographics in terms of user age, gender, location, and more. Use these demographics to determine if your potential customers use these sites. Social media might not be the best as a sole strategy for a start-up since you need fans, friends, and followers to be on the receiving end. But it might be a good strategy to sign up for all the major social media sites to reserve your name and then start using a few that best meet your needs. There is much buzz around social media—specific applications can be right for you, or they can become time consuming and take away time and energy from other more suitable marketing tools. In other words, adopt social media with your eyes wide open.

What do small businesses use social media marketing for? According to Wasp Barcode Technologies' 2016 "State of Small Business Report," following are the primary uses:

- **Promote a specific product/service:** 45%

- **Share information about promotions, sales, and discounts:** 38%

- **Gain likes and fans:** 38%

- **Solicit/respond to customer feedback:** 34%

- **Provide videos highlighting products/services:** 29%

- **Share a company post or blog:** 28%

- **Establish personal expertise:** 23%

- **Provide training videos for customers:** 18%

It bears repeating: Know your customers before you decide if social media is the right marketing tool for you. According to the survey, small companies report lower percentages in each category than larger businesses. And companies with 5 to 10 employees use social media sites less frequently than larger firms. While 16 percent of the respondents used no social media as part of their marketing strategy, for the smaller firms that do, usage was 28 percent and for the larger firms it was only 7 percent.

Internet Advertising

Word of mouth is often thought of as the best form of marketing, but it does not come free or without effort. How does the chain get started and then maintained? What incentives are provided to customers to make positive comments about their experience with your company? Who are the opinion leaders and early adopters among your targeted customer base?

- Conduct an internet or mass mailing campaign. Of course, you need an email list to send to, and it is illegal to use email lists without the recipients' permission. But you can build your own list. In fact, the best email list is a natural/organic list you grow yourself by collecting business cards and noting who visits your website. As an interim step, you can post, with permission, in other people's newsletters and provide some incentive for readers to connect to your website.

- Create and maintain a blog. Do you have the time, energy, and ideas to maintain a blog? A blog that is frequently updated and has many followers is an asset. Among other things, it assists in search engine optimization and is a good resource for email campaigns. But a blog that is rarely updated is a distracter because the information may be old (like the newest post advertising a sale you held three months ago), which reflects poorly on your business. Use "paid search" by buying keywords on Google, Yahoo, Bing, and other search engines. Do some research on keywords that are important to your business. Focus on words potential customers may use and not necessarily on what you would use. For many, buying keywords will be the most effective method, considering reach and cost, to start a marketing campaign. You can cap your budget by the amount you are willing to pay per click and thus the total spending level. Some research indicates that paid search is best for reaching about 3 percent of all potential customers who are ready to make a purchase. Know the economics of how much you earn from a sale and how much you will be paying for the paid search to ensure the sale meets your profitability criteria.

- Give discounts for new or repeat business, either at your location, on your website, or in conjunction with companies like Groupon, Living Social, or the many others in this space. Just make sure you understand the economics and how much money you will net after paying these companies and if you would have made the sale anyway without using this enticement. Conduct reference checks with users of these daily deal sites to ensure you will be pleased with the product and service.

Marketing using the internet is very prevalent and, for some companies, the only venue used. To learn more about how it generally works and the terminology used, read the marketing blogs at www.orangesoda.com, www.constantcontact.com, lynda.com, and many more.

PRICING AND PRICING PHILOSOPHY

An integral part of the marketing plan is determining your pricing philosophy. It is framed in relation to your competition and comes before developing your price list or menu. Pricing is an essential part of your brand strategy and company image. Entrepreneurs often say that as a home-based sole proprietorship, they have low direct costs and almost no overhead and, therefore, will have the lowest price. And this will be the key way to attract customers. However, experience repeatedly demonstrates that low price as the key product/service differentiator is a poor strategy. How many times have you heard "you get what you pay for"? Lowest price is frequently connected with low quality. If low pricing is your main competitive advantage and marketing strategy, then there is only one direction to go, and that is continued lower pricing, which, of course, leads to lower margins and probably lower cash flow.

Get to know the competition and their pricing patterns. Often this is straightforward if prices are listed. Other times you or a friend needs to pose as a buyer and find out. Go to a nearby city where you may not be considered a competitor and talk with similar businesses. While investigating competitors, think about what their reaction might be to you as a new market participant—often this reaction is lowering their prices, which was addressed in the competitive analysis discussion on page 95.

Also consider that there are several components to price—hard and soft. Hard pricing is the sales ticket. Soft pricing are all the items surrounding the sale like multiple payment methods, credit terms, return policy, rebates, VIP cards, delivery options, customization, and others.

The bottom line on determining your prices is that it is more art than science. On the low end, your prices are determined by your cost of doing business—hopefully you are charging at least as much as your costs, and in this scenario, you will break even. On the high end, your prices are determined by what the market will bear, and you know this from your knowledge of competitor pricing. Sometimes there are rough general formulas, like retail might be twice wholesale, otherwise known as a 100 percent markup. Or you might receive 50 to 65 percent of the retail price for items sold on consignment. Whatever price you charge initially, it does not have to be that price forever. Gas stations change their prices every day, and internet sales prices have the ability to change every minute. So experiment and see what works.

How to Calculate Your Pricing

This is how a consulting service, which bills by the hour, might determine their prices. From your financial information, gather: 1) the total wages of those involved in providing the consulting service; 2) the total wages for those who support these individuals (for example, accounting, marketing, and executive staffs—in fact, all other staff); 3) all employee benefits, which might be in the range of 25 to 33 percent of payroll; and 4) all selling, general, and administrative (SG&A) expenses (for example, rent, travel, supplies, IT, and marketing).

Add the total of the last three categories, and divide that figure by the total direct wages—this results in an overhead rate, which might be in the range of 100 to 150 percent. Then, for each consultant, take their total wages divided by the number of hours worked to get their hourly rate. (The standard is 2,080 hours in a year, less vacation time; for a single consultant firm, at least 25 percent of the time will be spent marketing, rather than consulting.) Multiply that figure by the overhead rate just calculated, then multiply again by a desired profit margin to get the hourly billing rate. Of course, this "bottom-up" approach to the desired rate must be compared with what competitors are charging. In formula terms, this calculation might look like this:

1. **Wages for All Consultants** = $500,000 (5 @ $100,000 each)

2. **A Consultant's Hourly Wage Rate** =
$$\frac{\text{Annual Wages}}{\text{Hours}} = \frac{\$100,000}{2,080} = \$48.08/\text{hr.}$$

3. **Total Overhead Costs** =
    + Total Indirect Labor Cost
    + Payroll/Employee Benefits
    + SG&A
    = $200,000 + $150,000 + $400,000 = $750,000

4. **Overhead Rate** =
    Total Overhead Costs/Consultant Wages
    = $750,000/$500,000 = 150%

If we stopped calculating at this point, we would have a billing rate of $120.20/hr. ($48.08 + $48.08 x 150%) for this consultant. This rate would recover his/her costs and all the support or indirect costs and would place the company in a break-even position. Breakeven is better than a loss, but it is not the goal. To generate positive cash flow, you need to add another factor representing profit:

5. Profit Margin = 20%
   (see Chapter 13 for typical industry profit margins)

Consultant's Billing Rate =
   Wage Rate + Overhead Rate + Profit Margin
   = $120.20 + $120.20 x 20%
   = $144.24

This is how a manufacturing company might determine its minimum price based on its costs.

From your financial information, gather: 1) the direct cost for each product, which may include production, labor, and freight; 2) the total wages for those who support the production process (for example, accounting, quality control, procurement, and executive staffs—in fact, all other staff); 3) all employee benefits, which might be in the range of 25 to 33 percent of payroll; and 4) all selling, general, and administrative (SG&A) expenses (for example, rent, travel, supplies, IT, and marketing). Add the total of the last three categories, and divide this figure by the total direct wages—this results in an overhead rate, which might be in the range of 100 to 150 percent. If there is just one product being produced, then all costs are assigned to that product. If there is more than one product, then there must be an allocation of costs. This can be based on the relative number of units produced, or the relative value of the items being produced, or any other factor deemed appropriate. Combine the direct costs and the overhead costs, then divide that figure by the number of product units to get the total cost per unit. As with the consulting business example above, add a profit factor. Repeating the caveat, this "bottom-up" approach on the desired rate must be compared with what competitors are charging. For all businesses, your price should be determined by your product's or service's position in the marketplace and what others are charging for similar products and services.

Knowing your product/service price is important when evaluating the financial impact of offering reduced prices. For example, you may be asked to donate products/services to a charity or decide to reduce or even give away products as a promotional campaign. See Chapter 31, "Gifts in Kind," for an in-depth discussion on giving away products/services for free.

Sometimes you have a good prospective customer you would like to sell to, but they do not have much cash to pay you. In lieu of payment, they offer to give you a little cash and some equity in their start-up business. Should you take the deal? Knowing your pricing and thus the value of the current and maybe future sales will help determine how much equity to ask for. See Chapter 30, "Deal or No Deal?" for an in-depth discussion on trading products/services for equity.

Key Lessons

✓ Effective marketing plans are developed through research and analysis and will change as business conditions change. Taking shortcuts to describe the market does not help you.

✓ Every business has competition. After all, all customers who might want your product or service today bought it or something like it from a competitor yesterday.

✓ Most customers do not progress directly from awareness of your company to buying your product. It is therefore critical to have a "funnel" of prospects and customers at each stage of the buy cycle. One common mistake many new businesses make is that they get busy with their first few clients and then neglect marketing and sales. Then they find themselves with an empty prospect list and many months of no income. A complete marketing plan ensures that each stage of the buy cycle has tactics to attract prospective clients and guides them to the next stage toward purchase.

✓ Determine the metrics—how will you measure the success of each marketing tactic?

✓ Determining your product or service price is as much art as it is science. Price should be consistent with your brand strategy, market factors, and your cost structure. A price is not forever; you can change it until you find what works best. This especially applies to internet businesses, which commonly use dynamic pricing.

List five things you are going to do to drive traffic to your door. For each one, note five specific action items to make it happen, along with the amount of time it will take, how much it will cost, and your sales expectations.

MARKETING ACTIVITY	ACTION ITEMS (5 for each)	COST	EXPECTED SALES

Allocate the total cost for each Marketing Activity to the months of the year, and this becomes your marketing budget to use in the financial section. Note separately the costs incurred before you open your doors for business (the start-up costs) and the costs incurred once your business is up and running as this information will be used in separate parts of your financial forecast as discussed in Chapter 13. This will provide information for your start-up expenses.

MARKETING ACTIVITY	MONTHLY COST												TOTAL
	1	2	3	4	5	6	7	8	9	10	11	12	

Add up the sales expectations, and this will be your sales forecast to use in your income and cash flow statements in the financial section. For the first year, list the amounts by month, and for years two and three, list the amounts by quarter.

MARKETING ACTIVITY	YEAR 1 SALES	YEAR 2 SALES	YEAR 3 SALES

Chapter 11

GO WITH THE FLOW

Detailing Your Operations

Think About It

Does my operations plan...

✓ Describe the flow of operations, from raw materials to finished goods, including sourcing, quality control, R&D, and inventory management?

✓ Include my business location(s) and attributes that make them appropriate? And if the location is to be owned or leased?

✓ Note required licenses and regulations, intellectual property obtained to protect my products and services, and other legal considerations?

✓ Describe the personnel needed to successfully operate the business and a timeline for their hiring?

✓ Describe hours of operation and other customer-facing activities?

This business plan section details how you will operate your business on a daily basis. It ensures all the resources necessary to run a successful operation have been considered and coordinated.

This includes such factors as location, equipment, leases, quality control, staffing, key vendors, hours of operation, inventory management, return policy, and, especially for internet businesses, your website strategy, privacy policy, and opt-in/out emails. Obviously for a home-based service business, many of these factors will not apply.

Production

How and where are your products or services produced? What is self-produced and what is purchased for resale? Explain your production techniques and costs, quality control, customer service, inventory control, product development, portion control (for restaurants), and so on. Are any products or raw materials imported? If so, how do you ensure quality, how do you arrange payment? Are any materials hazardous like dry cleaning, nail salon, or lawn care chemicals? Do you need special processing and equipment?

Location

If you have a specific location in mind, then state it; if not, give a general description of the location attributes you think are important. It is unlikely you will have a location when you start preparing your business plan as it is not financially prudent to buy or lease a property before you even know you have a feasible and viable business idea. Unfortunately, it will be difficult to obtain a bank loan without a specific location referenced, and conversely, it will be difficult to sign a lease agreement without having the funding in hand. Often these two paths close nearly on the same day. In the plan, include such things as the amount of space, building type, zoning, utilities, signage, access, parking, visibility to the street, traffic counts, and so forth. Also, include enough information about new building costs or the buildout of an existing space so when you get to the start-up costs in the financial section, you will have a basis to work from.

If you have a particular location in mind and it is vacant, find out who the previous tenants were, what type of businesses they had, and why they left. If the previous business is the same or similar to yours, have a serious conversation with yourself about why you are different and will be successful.

What will be your business hours, and how does this fit with both staff and customer needs?

With your knowledge of potential customers, you know how they like to shop. Do you have a B2B business where your product or service is purchased during normal business hours? How about a retail business—are purchases made from home, or while commuting to and from work? How about weekend sales? Remember, an internet-based business is 24/7.

Commercial Leases

Most likely, at start-up, you will lease rather than buy your office/store/factory, unless you are working from home. According to my SCORE-mentor colleague Richard Rose, who has been both a commercial space tenant and landlord, here is what to expect during the commercial lease process and what to be alert to.

- **Prepare.** Write a business plan with financial projections and a personal financial statement, then arrange for funding.

- **Engage a leasing agent.** The landlord will pay your leasing agent a commission; your agent only earns a commission if there's a deal and a separate agreement between you and your agent.

- **Discuss the criteria for your space with your agent.** What kind of business will you have? Where do you want the space to be located? What size space (in square feet) do you require, plus any special amenities/requirements? How much are you prepared to spend?

- **Investigate available spaces with your agent.** Check listings online and drive around areas of interest looking for vacant space. When you find a space of interest, your agent will arrange for you to see it and present you to the landlord's agent. If you have questions about a space, ask your agent.

- **Draw up a letter of intent (LOI) agreement.** Either the tenant or the landlord may start the LOI process, which includes a non-binding agreement stating the economic terms of the deal and other matters important to the tenant and the landlord. If all parties are in agreement, the landlord will prepare a lease that includes those terms.

- **Consult with an architect and general contractor.** During the negotiation of the LOI and lease, the tenant should obtain an estimate of the total buildout cost from an architect and a general contractor, who have knowledge of the local building/zoning and ADA requirements. You should know your expected costs before signing the lease.

- **Retain an attorney to negotiate the lease and guaranty.** Commercial leases are complex, and the negotiations can be intense. It is best to have your lawyer negotiate on your behalf.

IT'S LIKE THIS: A small chain of soup and salad restaurants in Washington, DC, worked out the specifics of their location in order to write their operations plan. The owners decided that the appropriate hours of operation for the location's demographics were from 7am to 2pm. Since they were only serving breakfast and lunch, they determined that only one staff shift was required during these hours.

IT'S LIKE THIS: A client has a passion for designing wedding dresses, but it is secondary to her full-time job. The solution was to create an exclusive brand image: Her store is open only by appointment during the week and to all on the weekends. To add to the exclusive image, her dresses and prices are at the high end of the competitive range and she only shows her creations at the best wedding dress expos. The part-time hours allow her to run her wedding dress business profitability without jeopardizing her full-time job.

IT'S LIKE THIS: A client was planning to open a flotation studio. She had done all the right steps, from engaging a leasing agent to research-ing acceptable locations. She started the LOI discussions with the land-lord through her leasing agent. As this type of business is relatively new, its full dimensions were not fully understood by the prospective landlord. Well into the process, he learned about how much water is involved and how it needs to be changed out after every customer visit. He wanted no part of this in his building. The client lost a lot of time and some funds in this aborted attempt to gain a commercial lease. For her next attempt, she now understood what was important to a landlord, mentioned the water matter upfront in a manner that demonstrated it was not an issue, and was able to secure the lease.

Legal Environment

Describe the following in this section: licensing and bonding require-ments, permits, any special regulations covering your industry or pro-fession, zoning or building code requirements, insurance coverage, trademarks, copyrights, and patents (pending, existing, or purchased).

You should know the requirements for doing business in your area—what business license, company and company name registration, and sales tax registration is required. A good source of this information is county economic development agencies as their purpose is to bring business to the area. For internet searches, a good search phrase is "how to do business in XX." It does not matter if the town is large or small—you will be able to find this information online. For example, when you do this search for a small town like Era, Texas, with a population of 99, you get redirected to the website for the State of Texas on how to start a business and receive the appropriate licenses and permits. Likewise, the rural town of Gouverneur, New York, with a population of about 4,000, has much information to provide. Larger cities have websites containing this information and where in their bureaucracy to go for the appropriate permits and licenses. Keep in mind, it usually takes longer than expected to secure all the needed licenses and permits.

IT'S LIKE THIS: A client couple wanted to start a violin and voice lessons business, and they wanted to call it a "school." However, in their area, state regulations have strict standards regarding "schools" so the clients called the business an "institute" and referred to what they did as "tutorial lessons." Other examples where states usually have extensive regulations are day care centers and almost anything to do with health care.

Personnel

Describe the number of employees, type of labor (skilled, unskilled, and professional), where and how you will find the right employees, and pay structure in enough detail to provide a basis for the payroll cost section of the financial statements.

Also include which positions will be staffed by employees (full and part time) and which by contractors. It is helpful to have a staffing timeline of when—usually tied to sales or production activity levels—you plan (need) to bring on additional staff. Some entrepreneurs want to be fully staffed from day one, but this is an expensive luxury—it is better to start small and grow.

What benefits will you provide? All employers are required to provide (contribute to) Social Security and Medicare. The employer cost of these two benefits is about 7.65 percent of payroll in 2016. To this, you will add the cost of federal and state unemployment insurance and discretionary benefits like medical and life insurance, vacation, 401(k) or other pension program, and so forth. Eventually you will need an employee handbook, which is as much to protect yourself regarding the terms and conditions of employment at your company as it is to make employees aware of these policies.

When considering how much to pay employees, don't forget about yourself. In a start-up, it is typical that the founder/CEO gets paid last, but, hopefully, still gets paid. See Chapter 28, "Pay Day," for an in-depth discussion on how much to pay yourself.

Many entrepreneurs want to start their business with independent contractors as they think this approach is cheaper than having full- or part-time employees. But the IRS has strict rules on what conditions of engagement meet the independent contractor arrangement and which meet the employee arrangement. The reason the IRS is interested is that they want to collect the payroll taxes. Because there is much misunderstanding on this subject, it is best to get the rules directly from the source. The following excerpt is from the IRS website (IRS.gov):

> As a small business owner you may hire people as independent contractors or as employees. There are rules that will help you determine how to classify the people you hire. This will affect how much you pay in taxes, whether you need to withhold from your workers' paychecks, and what tax documents you need to file.
>
> Here are seven things every business owner should know about hiring people as independent contractors versus hiring them as employees.
>
> **1.** The IRS uses three characteristics to determine the relationship between businesses and workers:

a. **Behavioral Control** covers facts that show whether the business has a right to direct or control how the work is done through instructions, training, or other means.

b. **Financial Control** covers facts that show whether the business has a right to direct or control the financial and business aspects of the worker's job.

c. **Type of Relationship** factor relates to how the workers and the business owner perceive their relationship.

2. If you have the right to control or direct not only what is to be done but also how it is to be done, then your workers are most likely employees.

3. If you can direct or control only the result of the work done—and not the means and methods of accomplishing the result—then your workers are probably independent contractors.

4. Employers who misclassify workers as independent contractors can end up with substantial tax bills. They can also face penalties for failing to pay employment taxes and for failing to file required tax forms.

5. Workers can avoid higher tax bills and lost benefits if they know their proper status.

6. Both employers and workers can ask the IRS to make a determination on whether a specific individual is an independent contractor or an employee by filing Form SS-8, "Determination of Worker Status for Purposes of Federal Employment Taxes and Income Tax Withholding," with the IRS.

7. You can learn more about the critical determination of a worker's status as an independent contractor or employee at www.IRS.gov by selecting the "Small Business" link. Additional resources include IRS Publication 15-A, *Employer's Supplemental Tax Guide*; Publication 1779, *Independent Contractor or Employee*; and Publication 1976, *Do You Qualify for Relief Under Section 530?* These publications and Form SS-8 are available on the IRS website or by calling 800-TAX-FORM.

But you are not finished learning about employee vs. independent contractor status and regulations. The Department of Labor (DOL), which is tasked with enforcement of the Fair Labor Standards Act, has its own criteria, which are slightly different from the IRS. See a blog on this subject at blog.dol.gov/2015/07/15/employee-or-independent contractor.

Inventory

Describe what kind of inventory you will keep, and whether it is raw materials, supplies, and/or finished goods, along with the average value in stock (in other words, what is your inventory investment), inventory turnover rate, and how this compares to industry averages, seasonal build-ups, and lead time for ordering. Often inventory is a large component of start-up costs as you need these supplies before you can make sales, particularly in a retail business. Inventory, especially if it is easily identified and has a ready market, might be used as collateral against a loan used to purchase it.

Credit Terms, Discounts, and Return Policies

Do you plan to sell to customers on credit, offer discounts, and allow returns? If so, under what conditions?

Suppliers

Identify any key suppliers and relationships/agreements you have or plan to have along with their reliability. Note if any suppliers are foreign, as well as arrangements for ordering, quality control, payment terms, return policy, and so on. Also, note if any letters of credit will be required, especially for international shipments.

Key Lessons

✓ Securing a business location and bank loan can be a frustrating process because the landlord wants to see the money first and the banker wants to see the lease first. This is a time-tested process, and each agreement closes at about the same time.

✓ Staffing with contractors rather than employees is not at your discretion. The company-staff relationship determines the IRS rules that apply—the more control exercised by the company, the more likely staff should be treated as employees rather than contractors.

✓ The design of your operations should be in sync with the customer need being fulfilled and company image.

Using the information in the chapter as a guide, write down your business's specifics pertaining to:

Production

Facility Locations

Intellectual Property

Leasing

Personnel and
Form of Engagement

Payroll

Inventory

Suppliers

Sales Terms

Chapter 12

TEAM PLAYERS

Who's on Your Management Team?

Think About It

Does my management team and organization (which might just be me)...

✓ Possess the skills and experience for this particular business?

✓ Include advisors and mentors?

✓ Include the "front line" positions of marketing and production as well as the "back office" positions like accounting and customer service?

✓ Have a board of directors if I am organized as a C, S, benefit, or nonprofit corporation?

✓ Have a board of advisors to assist me in areas where I do not have skills or experience and act as a sounding board?

With a limited track record and usually few assets, the early success of a small business is typically a "bet" on the entrepreneur. That makes this section very important as it must convince readers that the bet is a safe one. In some businesses, it takes two entrepreneurs to be successful where one is "Mr. Inside" and one is "Mr. Outside." For example, in restaurants, there needs to be a good chef as well as someone to manage the dining room and external marketing. Another example is in the temporary staffing business where one expertise is finding firms that need staffing and the other expertise is finding, vetting, and managing individuals who wish to be temporary staff.

Like the Product Development Roadmap discussed in Chapter 9, "Like No Other," you should have a team hiring plan that describes which functions/staff will be hired when—when is staff needed to design and implement the product and marketing strategies? This will be good input for the financial forecasts and again is a demonstration of how any funding will be used.

Include a one-page bio on each of the key people involved, which should be written in a style that demonstrates "been there, done that, and have the T-shirt." You want to demonstrate that you have the technical chops for the business as well as the leadership skills. Where there might be experience/skills gaps, note how you have added others to the team to provide this expertise. Note if any of your team has previously worked together.

These bios will help in developing the messaging about why customers should buy from you.

A classic mismatch is the programmer who is great at writing games or apps and is tired of his boss, so he wants to start his own company. The problem is, he may be IT proficient, but he has had a position where he always worked on what he was told to do, which means he did not have any leadership, marketing, finance, or other management experience. That translates to a difficult time obtaining a bank loan, or worse, not having the skills to run a business.

IT'S LIKE THIS: A client with a passion for a bakery-type retail store had put together an excellent business plan. He also had a good credit score, was prepared to personally invest more than 20 percent, and had collateral valued at 125 percent of the requested bank loan. However, he could not demonstrate in his bio that he had retail, food service, or related experience, and he did not have team members with these skills, so the bank said no to the loan application. Eventually he found sufficient funding from personal funds, family, and friends, and opened the store successfully.

IT'S LIKE THIS: The sales team of an established catering company saw potential in new markets that the owner would not consider, so they teamed up to start their own company. In the business plan, they provided excellent information on target markets, potential competitor reaction to a new company, and operating details. Plus, the plan was clearly and persuasively presented. However, they had not made the transition from marketers to owners who were concerned with all aspects of a business. Also, the presentation of the financial information was subpar—there was no mention in the executive summary of the amount of money being requested from the bank, no earnings potential to demonstrate they could repay the loan, and no statement of assumptions or financial statements for the three-year period. The clients updated the business plan, and then with good information about the business prospects, they could intelligently discuss and negotiate a lease agreement with the landlord. However, after all this work, they found they could not afford what was being asked by the landlord, so they walked away.

IT'S LIKE THIS: A senior marketing manager for a national company had been interested in yoga for many years and decided to open her own yoga studio. She thoroughly researched her target market and niche, developed detailed sales forecasts by service and product, knew her pricing philosophy and the competition. In the first draft of the business plan, she included most of the financial information in an appendix (just like a marketing person to bury the financial information). But she later revised the plan to include a full financial section (which demonstrated that finance is important to the owner) and developed a list of key assumptions used to generate the financial statements. Did she successfully make the transition from marketing executive to chief executive? Yes, she received the requested bank funding.

This management team section is a good place for a chart—an organizational chart. Of course, this implies several people in the company. A big mistake many start-ups make is forming a large organization with many players for a business where the funding is still in question. As we said before, the best plan is to start small and grow.

IT'S LIKE THIS: A client with a full-time, well-paying "day job" decided with colleagues to build and operate an environmentally friendly car wash and hire a brother-in-law to manage it. Often with start-ups, margins are thin, so it's best to operate a business alone; in addition, hiring family members is often a difficult situation. Sure enough, after nine months, they had to let the brother-in-law go.

How you will organize and staff your business to undertake marketing and sales should be addressed here or in the previous operations section. Will you be the chief salesperson, will you use independent reps, and will you have a part- or full-time person to help with social media and internet marketing?

If your company is organized as a C, S, or benefit corporation or a nonprofit, you will need a board of directors, set of bylaws, and all the other administrative and governance procedures that come with these organization types.

If you're structured as an LLC, it is your decision whether to have a formal board of directors or a more informal board of advisors, who can help in many ways. It's a good idea to include these people in a business plan to inform the reader that you have considered all aspects.

All companies can have a board of advisors—two to five professionals with a wide range of experiences to advise you on marketing, production, start-up, technology, customer access, finance, etc. They do not have any decision-making authority or fiduciary responsibility. They serve to assist you, and you can ignore their advice. Often they will serve without pay; in cases where they require compensation, you can provide a small ownership share (like one-quarter to one-half percent), since it is unlikely you will initially have cash to pay.

Either in this section or the previous one on operations, you should address how you will handle "back office" functions, particularly accounting and bookkeeping. It is important to communicate with potential funders that you have this critical area under control. Often in single-person start-ups, the entrepreneur takes on this role primarily because there is a shortage of funds to pay for help. However, most entrepreneurs start a company because they are good at selling, building, manufacturing, writing, and other functions, but accounting is not their strong suit. So if the entrepreneur has an extra hour each day, it is better spent doing more of what he/she is good at and what will bring in new customers and revenues and let someone else do the accounting. Even if you perform the weekly transaction accounting activities, consider hiring an accountant for your year-end financial statements and tax returns.

Sometimes you may need to find a business partner, a techie to assist with website development, or a co-owner to enhance your skills and experience. A place to find new team members is a website called CoFoundersLab.com, which bills itself as "Matchmaking for Entrepreneurs."

In summary, a business requires a team with a variety of skills and experiences to be successful. However, the team need not be all full-time employees, and in fact, it is typical for the start-up founder to initially be the sole full-time employee surrounded with this help.

Key Lessons

✓ Your bio should demonstrate you have the technical and leadership skills and industry experience to be successful—that you "have been there, done that, and have the T-shirt."

✓ Every entrepreneur and small business owner should surround themselves with advisors and mentors to assist in the many facets of knowledge and outreach needed to operate a small business successfully.

List your advisors and mentors:

Accountant	
Lawyer	
Insurance Agent	
Banker	
Mentor 1	
Mentor 2	
Advisory Board	
Board of Directors	
Key Staff	

Write your and any key staff's one-page bio, demonstrating experience and expertise in leadership and in your field of business.

Chapter 13

NUMBER SENSE

How to Prepare Your Financial Plan

Think About It

Does my financial plan...

✓ Contain a list of assumptions used to prepare the financial statements?

✓ Include those financial statements necessary for me to project and track my business and for a funder to evaluate my funding request?

✓ Incorporate information from all preceding business plan sections and is consistent with the executive summary content?

✓ Provide financial statements that depict believable results?

✓ Describe a business that I would invest my personal funds in?

One of the final elements in your business plan is the financial statements. While the financial plan is a very important section, it is appropriate for it to come last, because if the executive summary is a discussion of all that is to follow, the financial section is a recap of all that precedes it.

For many, tackling this section last is just fine because it is the one plan element that most entrepreneurs dread. They frequently feel like they have hit a wall when it comes to writing this section and they "blame" it for holding up their business plan. Typically this is because they do not understand it, or they are afraid of it, or they have made it unnecessarily difficult because they haven't carefully completed the rest of the business plan. Don't let this happen to you. Read through this chapter, and get free help from SCORE, an SBDC, a Women's Business Center, a county economic development center, or other resource. And, if all else fails, hire an accountant and financial planner to assist you.

IT'S LIKE THIS: A client had developed a web-based business and said she had hit a wall when it came to the finance section—all other sections of the plan were completed. The resolution should have been simple: Walk through the previous sections of the plan and pick out all the items necessary for the financial statements. But after a discussion of revenue and the assumptions the client had made regarding how she was going to get paid, the client admitted she had not yet figured this out—would it be subscription, advertising, an online store, or several other options? Once she worked through the other parts of the plan, the financial statements went together easily.

FINANCIAL ASSUMPTIONS

Financial statements are charts with lots of numbers and few words describing what they are all about. Therefore, it is advisable, if not mandatory, to have an introductory page in your financial plan noting in plain English the key assumptions and how each one was determined. If you can convince the reader about the reasonableness of the assumptions, then the "sale" has already been made when he/she reads the financial statements.

Most of the assumptions in this section will come from earlier sections of the business plan. For example, from the marketing section, you have the sales forecast and the marketing budget. From the management team and organization section, you get the staffing—number of people, hours worked, and pay rates. From the operations section, you have buildings/equipment used, rentals, utilities, and other facility costs.

There are many ways of developing the assumptions, with the two principal approaches being top down (macro) and bottom up (micro). Start with the bottom-up approach, since this will give support for the assumptions, and then compare these results to industry norms to see if they are realistic. It is easy to use a top-down macro approach and say the market is $15 billion in sales and all we are looking for is 1 percent. This sounds like a small amount, so funding should be a slam-dunk, but, in reality, you are just dreaming. Similarly, if you say we will make $150,000 in annual sales this year, then next year we should grow by 10 percent, to $165,000, that is a dangerous claim if there is no marketing plan to demonstrate this is achievable. So start with the basics. List your products and services, note how much you can produce/provide, and through the rigorous development of your marketing plan, state how much you can reasonably expect to sell. If you are doing this business plan for yourself, you can have several cases—most likely pessimistic and optimistic.

To test your bottom-up forecasts with reality, there is a free website for looking at profit margins by industry: www.bizstats.com. Another excellent source for checking the reality of your financial results relative to industry information is *Annual Statement Studies: Financial Ratio Benchmarks*, prepared by the Risk Management Association. You should be able to find this material at a bank's commercial lending department as well as in the business research section of a public library.

In the "Financial Statements" section, you will find an example of the three primary financial statements: profit and loss, cash flow, and balance sheet. To include numbers in these financial statements, we start with the following set of assumptions:

Sales (from your marketing section and summarized for this example)

- $300,000 in Year 1 and $500,000 in Year 2

Cost of Goods Sold (from your operations section and summarized for this example)

- **Product 1:** 35 percent in Year 1 and 30 percent in Year 2
- **Product 2:** 55 percent in Year 1 and 50 percent in Year 2

Expenses

- In Year 1, two full-time staff and one contractor while in Year 2, three full-time staff, increased pay for current staff, and two contractors
- Payroll taxes and benefits at 15 percent of compensation
- Leased facility with monthly rent of $4,000, increasing 4 percent each year (all per the lease)

Operational Financing

- Inventory is equal to 1½ times one month of cost of goods sold (COGS)
- Accounts receivables equal to approximately one-half of one month of sales
- Accounts payables equal to one-half of one month of COGS

Financing

- 7-year $100,000 bank loan at 7% simple interest
- $25,000 owner's contribution

- Start-up funding of $125,000 comprised of $80,000 to purchase equipment and building refurbishment; $15,000 for
  initial inventory; $18,000 for marketing, professional services,
  and deposit; and $12,000 for cash on hand

TIMELY MATTERS

How many years should be included in the forecasts? The standard
is three years of financial statement information, with the first year
by month and years two and three by quarter. This will help you
think of seasonality patterns. Sometimes banks ask for five years of
forward-looking information—and if it is required as part of a loan
application, you will submit it—but they recognize it is a pure guess-
work. If you have an existing business, then also include three years
of actual historical information. Banks and angels like to see this historical information by month to see what the cash "burn rate" has
been—how much cash you are spending a month and then compare
it to the forecast and note the changes. Also, for both existing and
start-up businesses, at a given monthly expenditure level, include
how long the requested amount of loan/equity will last and then
what your funding alternatives are.

Before you can provide any forecasts—in fact, before you can even
start the accounting process—you must select a fiscal year. All businesses have a fiscal year, and most often it is the calendar year. You
should select a fiscal year that follows any natural business cycle. For
example, businesses associated with schools often adopt the school
calendar so their fiscal year ends on June 30. Businesses associated
with the federal government often adopt the federal fiscal year, ending on September 30. Many retail businesses that do a substantial
portion of their annual sales during the December holidays and
January clearance sales often adopt a late January or early February
fiscal year. Some businesses adopt a fiscal year starting on the date
they opened their business, say August 1.

If you have a start-up and have not yet selected a fiscal year and there
is no compelling reason not to have a fiscal year ending on December

31, then use the calendar year as your fiscal year. This means that your first year will be a "short" year—from the date you start to the calendar year end. For most, this will align your business year with the way you file taxes on your personal IRS Form 1040, which is on a calendar-year basis. The following year will have the full 12 months. A small business is hard enough to "sell" when pitching for a loan or a big contract. You do not need to spend the extra time explaining why you are using a fiscal year different than the calendar year.

Procter & Gamble and Microsoft have fiscal years ending on June 30, but they are in a different league. Sole proprietorships and business organizations taxed as sole proprietorships must elect a business fiscal year the same as their personal fiscal year, which for most of us is the calendar year.

Once you have adopted a fiscal year, it is possible to change it, though you will need to demonstrate how the change will improve financial reporting (and not tax minimization). You will also need to file IRS Form 1128, "Application to Adopt, Change, or Retain a Tax Year." In some cases, there might be a fee to make this change.

FINANCIAL STATEMENTS

The three primary financial statements are income statement, cash flow statement, and balance sheet. In addition, a list of start-up expenditures and, in some cases, a break-even analysis are helpful additions.

Frequent questions from business plan writers are where do the line item names in each of the financial statements come from, is there a standard financial statement template for all businesses, and how much detail should be shown in the financial statements? There is no fixed financial statement template that applies to all businesses. The line items should be what are important for you to track business activity to know you are headed in the right direction. Make no mistake, all transactions will be recorded, but the line on which they are reported is somewhat up to you. For example, is it important to list separately various types of labor compensation or details of marketing expenditures or technology costs?

If you are using one of the accounting software products, when you open the box and insert the disc or download the application from the vendor's website, there will be a series of questions about your business, and based on the vendor's experience, they will offer a format—in essence your chart of accounts. Installing this accounting software is your first accounting system. You might be thinking, "Should I be hiring a CFO, an accountant, and/or a bookkeeper?" Likely, at the outset, you do not have the funds to make these hires—the need for these excellent resources will come when your business grows. See Chapter 29, "Call in the Financial Pros," for an in-depth discussion on when to hire this talent.

On the following pages are the traditional financial statements in the order commonly displayed in business plans for companies that have been in business for some time. So if you have an established business, you should follow this guide, and if you have an established nonprofit, you should follow the comparable guide for nonprofits discussed more in Chapter 15.

If you are a small start-up, then in your feasibility study and early drafts of your business plan, start with the cash flow statement shown and discussed on pages 148 to 150. This should provide the most useful information early in your business start-up. As your planning develops, in later drafts of the business plan, add the income statement and finally the balance sheet. Two reasons to include the balance sheet earlier: If you provide credit terms for sales, you will want to track accounts receivable (amount customers owe you), or if you receive credit terms from vendors, you will want to track accounts payable (amount you owe vendors), which are two line items found on the balance sheet.

Income Statement

The income statement has many aliases and all are acceptable: income statement, profit and loss statement, P&L, statement of income, statement of operations, statement of operations and comprehensive income, statement of earnings, and, if you have a nonprofit, statement of activities.

This statement shows the amount of income/earnings generated over a period of time, whether that is a month, a quarter, or a year. It starts with revenues, which are the amount of sales (often called the top line), then lists the costs incurred in making those sales, and after subtracting the costs from the revenues, notes the income or earnings. In simplest terms, the income statement starts with the money you earn by selling products and services, so you first list products/services, number of units sold, and price per unit achieved, which can also be written as volume times price equals revenue. The second category contains the direct costs incurred to produce the products sold—the supplies and the manufacturing costs if you make the product or the purchase cost if you resell a product. These expenses are called variable costs as they change in direct proportion to the amount produced. They are included in a section called "cost of goods sold." The third category on the income statement is for all other costs; usually these are fixed costs and include such items as rent, insurance, utilities, staff payroll, benefits, marketing, advertising, travel, use of consultants, etc.

To prepare this statement according to accounting conventions, you must decide whether to use the cash or accrual basis of accounting. This is an appropriate subject for accounting books, but suffice it to say that cash accounting is the way many small businesses start as it is intuitively obvious to the non-accountant. However, it is simplistic, does not provide the best information for managing the business, and is not a method from which you can achieve a "clean" audit opinion, if you are in a business or nonprofit that needs audited financial statements. Accrual accounting is the preferred method for established businesses. If you seek funding from a bank or angel investor, you should present your income statement using the accrual method. For businesses that have inventory and average annual gross receipts greater than $10 million, the IRS generally requires you to use the accrual method of accounting.

IT'S LIKE THIS: A specialty food manufacturer and distributor used cash accounting and recorded the cost of inventory and packaging when paid for, which was once a quarter. When the company looked at its monthly financial statements, the results were highly variable, due to its accounting methods, not operations. For example, for two months of the quarter, gross margins were 65 percent while for the third month, they were 5 percent. The company switched to accrual accounting so their financial reports more appropriately matched their business operation.

Businesses organized as sole proprietorships, limited liability companies (LLCs), or subchapter S corporations have several options on how to be taxed, but almost all entrepreneurs elect for the company to be a "pass through." If you recall from Chapter 8, what this means is that while the company prepares a tax return to the IRS, it is for information purposes only and no payment is provided. The owners are provided information on their share of the financial results, and they include this information on their personal tax return. Thus, when preparing the company income statement for one of these three legal structures, the "bottom line" should come before federal and state income tax as these will be paid by the owners and not the company. This applies only to federal and state income taxes. Sales tax, payroll tax, personal property tax, real estate tax, and other similar operational taxes are the company's responsibility to report and pay. If you have a C corporation, then the "bottom line" is shown after federal and state income tax, since the C corporation is an income tax payer.

Another consideration in preparing an income statement is how to report interest expenses from an anticipated loan. This is a business expense, but if you are preparing financial statements as part of a loan application, you do not want to start "negotiating with yourself." What if you assume a five-year, $100,000 loan at 8 percent interest and the bank is willing to provide $100,000 over seven years at 7 percent? In drafts, prepare the income statement with the loan interest included so you know if the company will be financially

MY BEST COMPANY
Income Statement
For the Year Ended December 31, 20XX

	YEAR 1	YEAR 2	
Revenues			
Sales of Product 1	$300,000	$500,000	
Sales of Product 2	400,000	800,000	
Other Revenues	10,000	12,000	
Total Revenues	**$710,000**	**$1,312,000**	
Cost of Goods Sold			
Cost of Product 1	$105,000	$150,000	
Cost of Product 2	220,000	400,000	
Total Revenues	**$325,000**	**$550,000**	
Gross Profit	**$385,000**	**$762,000**	**58%**
Expenses			
Compensation	$150,000	$254,500	
Payroll Tax and Benefits	22,500	38,175	
Consultants and Contractors	50,000	90,000	
Rent	48,000	49,920	
Marketing and Advertising	40,000	40,000	
Supplies	20,000	20,000	
Printing and Postage	10,000	15,000	
Utilities	6,000	7,000	
Dues and Subscriptions	5,000	5,000	
Website Support	7,500	7,500	
Equipment Maintenance	2,000	2,000	
Insurance	5,000	5,000	
Taxes (Not Income Taxes)	4,000	4,000	
Miscellaneous	4,000	5,000	
Depreciation	8,000	8,000	
Total Expenses	**$382,000**	**$551,095**	
Operating Income/(Loss)	**$3,000**	**$210,905**	
Interest Expense	$7,000	$7,000	
Income Taxes (Fed and State)	(1,400)	71,367	
Net Income/(Loss)	**($2,600)**	**$132,538**	**10%**

viable, since interest expense is a real cost, but in the version provided to the bank, take it out.

On the previous page is a typical income statement for a company organized as a C corp, since this has the most line items (note: the two rows that show percentages will be discussed later).

Two years are shown in this example, but for your business plan, show the number of years required by your banker or other funder. In an appendix, show the first year by month. If you have been in business for some time, you would typically show three years of actual results as well.

Once your business has started, you will produce a monthly income statement. The first column showing the line items being tracked will not change; however, the columns of numbers will. It's typical to show both current month and year-to-date information and, in some cases, a comparison to last year. Of more importance is showing actual performance compared to a budget; from this comparison and analysis, you can judge if you are on track with your plans. Your first budget is the monthly detail shown in the business plan. A typical income statement format could look like this for the month of August:

MY BEST COMPANY
Income Statement
For August 2013

	AUGUST 2017			AUGUST 2017 YTD			AUG 2016
	Actual	Budget	Variance	Actual	Budget	Variance	Actual
Revenue							
Cost of Goods Sold							
Gross Profit							
Expenses							
Operating Income/ (Loss)							

Income is the most common measure of financial performance. When reading the newspaper or hearing a radio or TV business report, it is a company's income/earnings that are being reported. And for publically traded companies, it will be based on the number of common shares outstanding and become earnings per share.

In the income statement, it is common for there to be just a few lines tracking the products and services sold and many more lines tracking the expenses incurred to produce and sell these products and services. Some find it useful to group these expenses by their relationship to the products and services; the key is, are the expenses variable to the number of products or services sold or are they fixed regardless of the sales volume? Eventually all expenses are variable as staff level or marketing activities can always change, so consider this just over a year's time. In the sample income statement, the cost of producing the product is shown separately as it is variable to the number of products sold.

The sample income statement on page 144, while generic to all business types, includes categories like cost of goods sold, which is used by companies with manufacturing and/or inventory. Following is an income statement format that might be used by a service company, like the consulting firm used in the pricing strategy discussion in Chapter 10. For this type of enterprise, there are few forms of revenue, but managing people and facilities costs is important.

MY BEST CONSULTING COMPANY
Income Statement
For the Year Ended December 31, 20XX

Revenues

Consulting to Government Agencies $

Consulting to For-Profit Businesses

Consulting to Nonprofits   _____

Total Revenues

Expenses

   Total Direct Labor

   Total Indirect Labor

Employee Benefits

   Payroll Taxes

   Vacation/Sick/Holiday

   401(k)

   Health, Life, and Disability Insurance

   Workers' Compensation   _____

   Total Employee Benefits

Selling, General, and Administrative Expenses (SG&A)

   Insurance

   Equipment Rental and Maintenance

   Rent

   Computer Software

   Website Hosting

   Telephone and Utilities

   Postage and Freight

   Printing

   Office Supplies

   Recruiting

   Subscriptions

   Travel

   Meals and Entertainment

   Licenses and Registrations

   Vehicle

   Marketing

   Advertising

   Legal and Accounting

   Depreciation

   Operational Taxes

   Other   _____

   Total SG&A   _____

Total Expenses   _____

Profit Before Interest and Income Taxes $

Cash Flow Statement

The cash flow statement has few aliases. Similar to the income statement, it is the amount of cash flow generated by the company over a particular period of time. It reports the cash generated from the company's operations, investing, and financing activities. In some ways, the cash flow statement is more inclusive than the income statement as it includes capital expenditures for equipment and buildings that will benefit the company for many years as well as loans and their repayments, which may provide the financial resources to successfully operate the business.

For a small business, income is "nice" and fits with common usage, but it is cash flow that puts food on the table. When you get into the details of computing an income statement, you will find that the accounting conventions include some "non-cash" events or change the timing of when cash is spent and when it is reported. So it is the cash flow statement that should reconcile to your bank account balance. To be blunt, in a small business you need to manage for the cash results. See Chapter 27, "Are You Liquid?" for a more in-depth discussion on how much cash to keep in your business.

A cash flow statement has three general categories: cash flow from operations, cash flow from investments, and cash flow from financing. Following is a description of each category:

- **Cash flow from operations** is where 95 percent of all transactions will occur and represents the ongoing, day-to-day business activities. These are the repetitive transactions of producing a product or service, selling it, and getting paid. This is the cash-generating power of your business and needs to be a positive number.

- **Cash flow from investments** contains those few transactions where you spend capital for the long-term improvement of the business—the business will usually benefit from these investments several years down the road. These might be the purchase of a building or the buildout of a store, manufacturing and IT equipment, vehicles, etc. As investments, these are a use of cash. In the case where you sell such items, it will be a source of cash. For a small business, many of these types of purchases occur at start-up.

- **Cash flow from financing** includes loans and their repayment as well as capital infusions from original owners and subsequent equity investors and the payment of dividends or distributions to the owners.

At the end of the cash flow statement is a tabulation of the starting cash position, the total cash generated during the period, and the ending cash position. The final amount shown should be the same as what is in your business bank account.

Mentioned earlier, and again here for emphasis, bankers and angels focus on the cash "burn rate"—how much cash is spent each month, quarter, and year? They want to see how the amount changes over time, and most important, how long the current funding will last. If you do not become cash flow positive with the use of the acquired funds, then what happens? If you are a banker, you are concerned there will be need for another loan and then there will be more liens on the business. If you are an angel investor, you are concerned there will be another equity funding round and your interest will be diluted. If the business is growing and gaining market traction, there will be a need for additional financing.

MY BEST COMPANY
Cash Flow Statement
For the Year Ended December 31, 20XX

	YEAR 1	YEAR 2
Cash Flow from Operations		
Revenues	$687,000	$1,280,333
Expenditures		
Inventory	$352,083	$568,750
Compensation	150,000	254,500
Payroll Tax and Benefits	22,500	38,175
Consultants and Contractors	50,000	90,000
Rent	48,000	49,920
Marketing and Advertising	40,000	40,000
Supplies	20,000	20,000
Printing and Postage	10,000	15,000
Utilities	6,000	7,000
Dues and Subscriptions	5,000	5,000
Website Support	7,500	7,500
Equipment Maintenance	2,000	2,000
Insurance	5,000	5,000
Taxes (not income taxes)	4,000	4,000
Misc.	4,000	5,000
Interest	7,000	7,000
Income Taxes	(1,400)	71,367
Total Expenditures	$731,683	$1,190,212
Cash Flow from Operations	**($44,683)**	**$90,121**
Cash Flow from Investments		
Fixed Asset Purchases	($80,000)	$0
Cash Flow from Investments	**($80,000)**	**$0**
Cash Flow from Financing		
Bank Loan Taken/(Paid)	$100,000	($15,000)
Owner's Contribution	25,000	0
Cash Flow from Financing	**$125,000**	**($15,000)**
Total Cash Flow	**$317**	**$75,121**
Beginning Cash	**0**	**317**
Ending Cash	**$317**	**$75,438**

Balance Sheet

The third financial statement is the balance sheet. Its primary alias is the statement of financial position; if you have a nonprofit, this is the statement title you should use. Unlike the income and cash flow statements, which show results over a period of time, the balance sheet is a snapshot of the assets, liabilities, and equity of the business at a singular point in time (i.e., on a specific date, such as the last day of the month, the last day of the quarter, or the last day of the year).

For assets, there are two general categories. The first is called current assets, which include items that are currently cash or can be converted into cash in the next 12 months; examples include cash, accounts receivable, and inventory. The second type is called fixed assets; examples include equipment, vehicles, buildings, building improvements, and land. Similarly for liabilities, obligations that are due within the next 12 months are called current liabilities; examples include staff payroll and money owed to vendors for recent purchases. Those with longer maturities are called long-term liabilities, such as long-term loans. Equity is the difference between assets and liabilities; in other words, after all the bills have been paid, any value remaining belongs to the owners. From an investment perspective, equity is the amount the owners have contributed to the business, plus any business value growth.

You have likely heard terms like "double-entry bookkeeping" or "the books are in balance." Often, these refer to total assets being equal to the sum of liabilities and equity. From your algebra book:

Total Assets = Total Liabilities + Equities

For the equation to remain in balance, if a change is made to one side of the equal sign, then an equal amount of change needs to be made to the other side.

In the balance sheet that follows, the assets are shown on the top and liabilities and equity at the bottom. You can also show these side by side so it is more visually apparent that the two sides are in balance.

MY BEST COMPANY
Balance Sheet
For the Year Ended December 31, 20XX

	YEAR 1	YEAR 2
Current Assets		
Cash	$317	$75,438
Accounts Receivable	23,000	54,667
Inventory	40,625	68,750
Total Current Assets	**$63,942**	**$198,855**
Fixed Assets		
Equipment	$80,000	$80,000
Cumulative Depreciation	8,000	16,000
Net Fixed Assets	**$72,000**	**$64,000**
Total Assets	**$135,942**	**$262,855**
Current Liabilities		
Accounts Payable	$13,542	$22,917
Long-Term Liabilities		
Bank Loan	$100,000	$85,000
Total Liabilities	**$113,542**	**$107,917**
Equity		
Capital Stock	$25,000	$25,000
Retained Earnings	(2,600)	129,938
Total Equity	**$22,400**	**$154,938**
Total Liabilities and Equity	**$135,942**	**$262,855**

Start-Up Expenditures

Start-up expenditures include all the costs incurred before you can open your door for business, or, in the case of an ongoing business, all the costs necessary before a new project can be launched. These costs will demonstrate much of what a loan or equity infusion will be used for, so detail is good. Start-up costs cover pre-opening expenditures, including marketing, legal, and accounting assistance; insurance premiums; rent and utility deposits; website development; computer and printer purchases; building/store purchase; improvements made to a leased or purchased facility; equipment or vehicles purchased; and opening inventory. An internet search using "start-up costs for XXX" will provide many resources. If funding comes from a bank, lenders will want to know how their money is being spent to ensure all the requested funds go into the business and not a spur-of-the-moment vacation you may decide to take.

In early drafts of your feasibility study and business plan, you can make educated guesses on the cost of these items. As the business plan matures, you should get several estimates for the higher-valued items. This is for your benefit since getting ready to open your business is usually your first experience in managing money and you must have your eye on the cash register.

Reality rarely turns out exactly as drawn up in a plan. While there is the potential of having "upside" surprises—meaning, you do not need as much funding as originally thought—it is the "downside" situations you need to be prepared for. Many entrepreneurs provide a contingency line item, either one overall amount or one for each of the major items. The amount of the contingency is dependent on your assessment of the risks involved. Typical contingency amounts are in the range of 5 to 20 percent.

Following is what a list of start-up expenditures might look like using the assumptions noted on page 138.

MY BEST COMPANY
Start-Up Expenditures

Remodeling Rented Store Space

Flooring	$12,000
Walls and Shelving	15,000
Electical	10,000
Plumbing	15,000
Total Refurbishment	**$52,000**

Equipment

Machine 1	$15,000
Machine 2	10,000
Computer and Printer	3,000
Total Equipment	**$28,000**

Total Inventory	**$15,000**

Marketing

Website	$5,000
Brochures	3,000
Total Marketing	**$8,000**

Professional Services

Accounting	$2,000
Legal	2,000
Total Professional Services	**$4,000**

Facilities

Rent Deposit	$4,000
Utility Deposit	2,000
Total Facilities	**$6,000**

Total Start-Up Expenditures	**$113,000**
Cash on Hand	**$12,000**
Total Funding	**$125,000**

You should keep all the details behind these numbers for your own records and in case the bank or investors asks for more information.

A second chart to prepare for yourself tracks cumulative cash flow. That way, you can determine how long it will be before the business is cumulative cash flow positive. The chart could look something like the one below. The amount shaded in gray is the total amount of negative cash (expenditures higher than receipts) and is the minimum amount of funding you will need to provide, either from yourself or from other sources like a bank. The information comes directly from the monthly projected cash flow statements and is a good way to visualize the results.

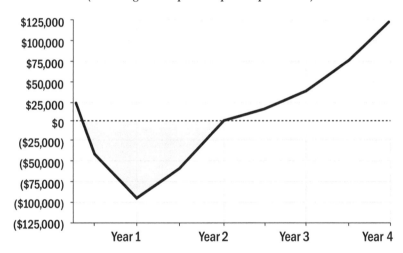

MY BEST BUSINESS
Cumulative Cash Flow
(Including Start-Up and Capital Expenditures)

The cumulative cash flow chart represents the reality that many businesses are not cumulatively cash flow positive for several years after start-up. There is a tension in that entrepreneurs are reluctant to show that their business idea follows this pattern, and thus they tend to use more robust assumptions, especially relating to sales volumes. The danger is that these entrepreneurs will overstate early-year sales and thus understate funding needs, with the result that they are under-capitalized from the beginning.

On Target?

The first time you put together your business plan financial statements you will probably not like the results. One way to assess your comfort level with the projected financial results is to have a goal in mind—for example, you need $70,000 annual cash flow by the third year to have sufficient funds to maintain a particular lifestyle, pay bills, save for retirement, and so on.

If your financial statements show that you will not meet your goal, go back to your financial assumptions page, which gathered the key information from the preceding sections, and see what might be changed. Of course, you can change items at will and get a result you like, but you may be fooling yourself. If you change a key assumption, make sure there is an analysis that supports it.

As you refine your financial statement assumptions and recalculate the financial results, make sure there is consistency between what you may be asking for in funding and what your financial statements say you need. In our example at the beginning of this chapter, we said we needed $100,000 from the bank and $25,000 from the owner's contribution. From the cash flow statement and balance sheet, we see that at the end of Year 1, we have a cash balance of only $517 and provided no contingency. So $125,000 in initial funding might not be quite enough.

This addresses the target in your business plan. Subsequently, you will have annual targets for operating and financial results. See Chapter 26, "Looking Ahead," for an in-depth discussion on how to set up and maintain a budget. Your business plan financial statements (with their assumptions) is your first budget.

Financial Ratios

Conventional wisdom states that at this point you should also include many financial ratios to demonstrate an informed analysis of your business against industry benchmarks. If your financial projections are in line with industry averages, fewer questions are asked by funders than if your numbers are an outlier. But the number of needed financial ratios is greatly overstated; all you need are a gross margin percentage, a net margin percentage, and, if you have inventory, something like inventory turns.

Gross profit percentage (alias gross margin percentage) is calculated from the income statement and/or cash flow statement and is found by dividing revenues less cost of sales by revenues. So for the income statement shown on page 144, it is:

$$\frac{\text{Revenues} - \text{COGS}}{\text{Revenues}} = \frac{\$1,312,000 - \$550,000}{\$1,312,000} = \frac{\$762,000}{\$1,312,000} = 58\%$$

What this means is that for every $100 of sales, you have $58 left to cover selling, general, and administrative expenses, plus profit. This is after subtracting the $42 to supply the product. When compared to other industry players, this measure is an indication of how good your manufacturing costs are or, if you purchase for resale, your vendor prices.

Obviously, for "idea" businesses like consulting and other similar services, which do not have a cost of goods sold section on their income statements, this ratio has no meaning. Of course, these types of businesses have expenses, but they are usually reported in the general expense section of the income statement. One exception might be if contractors are employed specifically for a customer assignment.

Net margin percentage is also calculated from the income statement and/or cash flow statement and is found by dividing net profits by revenues. So for the income statement shown on page 144 it is:

$$\frac{\text{Net Profit}}{\text{Revenues}} = \frac{\$132,538}{\$1,312,000} = 10.1\%$$

What this means is that for every $100 in sales, you have earned $10.10 after all costs. Do you think this is a good percentage? Let's compare it to some industry norms. Following is a list of net margins for a representative group of publicly traded companies, the results of which do

2015 Net Margin Percentage for Selected Companies

RETAIL	PERCENT (%)
Safeway and Kroger	1
Lowes	4
Wal-Mart	3
Home Depot	8
Nordstrom's	4
Starbucks	14
McDonald's	18
INDUSTRIAL AND GOVERNMENT CONTRACTORS	**PERCENT (%)**
Booz Allen Hamilton *(consulting)*	4
SAIC	3
Lockheed Martin	8
Honeywell	13
Caterpillar Tractor	4
John Deere	7
United Technologies	14
General Electric	5
ExxonMobil	6
Chevron	3
3M	16
Norfolk Southern Railroad	15
CONSUMER PRODUCTS	**PERCENT (%)**
Kellogg	5
Kimberly Clark	6
Pepsi	9
Disney	17
Colgate	10
TECHNOLOGY	**PERCENT (%)**
IBM	16
Google/Alphabet	23
Microsoft	13
Facebook	21
Apple	23
PHARMACEUTICALS	**PERCENT (%)**
Pfizer	14
Johnson & Johnson	22
Celgene	17
Lilly	12

not change much year to year. Information was taken from the companies' Form 10K filed with the Securities and Exchange Commission; no adjustments have been made and results have been rounded. Notice that companies with large federal government business have single-digit net margins.

There are two operational ratios that, if applicable to your business, might be instructive in making comparisons with industry norms. If you include these in your business plan, you will need to be prepared to discuss why you are more or less than the industry. It is part of the believability testing.

Inventory turnover or inventory turns measures how much inventory you have on hand to support a particular level of sales. Since in most cases you pay for raw materials before collecting cash from finished product sales, the more you have in inventory, the more of your own cash you are using. Lower inventory levels are better as long as you do not run short. Inventory turnover measures how many times a company's inventory is sold and replaced over a period and is generally calculated in a simplistic way as sales divided by average inventory. From the income statement and balance sheets shown previously, we have:

$$\frac{\text{Cost of Goods Sold}}{\text{Average Inventory}} = \frac{\$550,000}{(\$40,623+\$68,760)/2} = \frac{\$550,000}{\$54,692} = 10$$

This calculation shows that company turns over its inventory 10 times a year or almost once a month. How does this compare to competitors? Is there a short shelf life? How much effort is expended in frequent reordering?

Day's sales outstanding measures how your customers pay relative to credit terms you granted them. Since the transaction has been completed and you have incurred all the costs necessary to make the transaction, you want to make sure your customers pay when they agreed to pay. In essence, when a customer takes a product or service and agrees to pay at a later date, they are giving you an IOU, which you record in your accounting system as an account receivable. How are you doing on collecting these IOUs? The days sales outstanding, or DSO ratio, is calculated by dividing accounts receivable by sales and then multiplying by number of days in the period—usually a year. From the income statement and balance sheet on pages 144 and 152, the annual DSO is calculated like this:

$$\frac{\text{Accts Receivable}}{\text{Revenues}} \times 365 = \frac{\$54,667}{\$1,312,000} \times 365 = .0417 \times 365 = 15.2 \text{ days}$$

On average, if you give your customers 30 days to pay, they are paying early, but if you give them 10 days to pay, they pay late. Do you have a late payment charge to encourage payment on due dates? The results of this ratio can vary month to month given seasonality and level of sales. It is a good idea to measure monthly and watch the trend. You would not include this ratio in a business plan for a start-up, since you have no experience with customer payment terms; instead, you will assume that customers pay on time.

IT'S LIKE THIS: A client with a banquet hall and catering business provided a business plan, which included purchasing the venue and hosting a wide range of events. Included on the last page were 20 ratios calculated for the business. The client did not know what they meant or how they compared with industry norms, but he thought they were required and felt they gave the impression he had his hands on the issues. For a small start-up business, use just a few, if any, ratios. And if you use them, make sure you know what they mean and how they compare with industry norms.

Break-Even Analysis

This is a powerful tool to understand what amount of sales is necessary to break even. However, although this is a standard objective, breaking even should not be your goal. Break-even analysis is best used as a tool to ensure that the resources needed to produce revenue are in sync. You can do an internet search on how to calculate break-even points. In the traditional break-even analysis, you solve for the amount of sales required to break even. In the following "It's Like This," we used the desired level of sales and worked backward to determine how many resources—people—were required to achieve those sales.

IT'S LIKE THIS: A client's business idea was to be in the laundry business but own no facilities. He would collect laundry from area households, take it to a laundry facility, and, after cleaning, return it to the household. He researched the market, and after considering average size of washings, prices he could charge clients, and cost the facility would charge him, he thought he could clear $6 per load. When asked about his goals, he said that he would like to quit his current job and replace his $75,000 salary. Doing the math, at $6 per load, this would equate to 12,500 loads per year or 1,041 loads per month and about 47 loads per weekday. For each one of these loads, there is a pick up and a return delivery, or about 100 stops per day, which are probably concentrated in a few hours at the beginning and end of each day. In addition to making these stops, he would need time to take calls and solve problems. As a one-person operation, he did not have the time to accomplish all these tasks, and to add staff would change his basic financial results assumption. The client decided his idea was not economically viable.

IT'S LIKE THIS: A client had a special recipe for making chocolate chip cookies that she wanted to sell through Whole Foods. One type of chocolate chip cookies sold for $4 per pound at Whole Foods. The client was informed that Whole Foods operated on an average gross margin of 33 to 35 percent. This gross margin included the cost of goods purchased from suppliers and their space rental costs. This meant that if the client was successful in selling to Whole Foods, the price she would receive would be closer to $2.50 per pound. The client had a personal financial goal of earning $40,000 per year, so she would have to sell $100,000 of cookies per year. This would mean making 40,000 pounds of cookies per year, or 20 pounds of cookies every hour, based on an eight-hour day. The client was asked to determine if this was something she could do with her home kitchen or if she would have to go to a commercial kitchen. A commercial kitchen would result in rental expenses and probably some additional staffing, all of which would take away from the client's $40,000 annual earnings target.

IT'S LIKE THIS: A client with previous experience as a chef wanted to open a restaurant and had looked at a location with 2,000 square feet of space and an annual lease of $80,000. An industry rule of thumb is that, except in very prime locations, the rental expense should normally be within the range of 6 to 10 percent of the projected revenues. Since his location was not a prime one, the client would have to realize an annual revenue of $1.2 million for his restaurant to be profitable, or at least $100,000 per month. His menu projected an average customer check of $15, and his seating capacity was 60. This meant he would need full-capacity seating in three sittings every day of the week. This appeared to be highly optimistic, given his location and menu. The client decided to look for alternative locations, develop a menu that would result in a higher average check, and consider take-out and delivery services to improve his revenues.

Financial Statement Templates

Entrepreneurs looking for financial statement templates will find hundreds using a general internet search. As we discussed in Chapter 3, if you get counseling from a SCORE mentor, you will likely you use the free SCORE templates. Go to www.score.org, click on "Tools," then "Business Planning," then on "Business Plans & Financial Statements Template Gallery." Some clients choose to buy either LivePlan or Business Plan Pro, both by Palo Alto Software at www.paloalto.com/business_plan_software, and use it in conjunction with the SCORE templates.

REALITY CHECK

Once you have a set of financial statements that are consistent with all the research and components of your business plan, take a pause and conduct a "reality check." For example:

- Is there any business seasonality, and is it reflected in the monthly income and cash flow numbers?

- Are your gross/net margins in the competitive range? If not, why not? What is unique about your business?

- Are growth in number of customers and revenue supported by action plans and consistent with industry growth rates, or is all your growth achieved by taking business away from others?

- What are the risks to achieving your projected sales, income, and cash flow? Are these reasonable risks? Should contingencies be included?

- Is the amount of any requested funding supported by the needs shown in the financial statements?

IT'S LIKE THIS: A client with a convention, expo, and event planning business prepared a business plan and stated in the executive summary they needed $300,000 in funding and were prepared to self-invest $100,000, leaving $200,000 for a bank loan. So far so good as they were contributing 33 percent, which is more than most banks require. However, the projected financial statements showed being $600,000 profitable in the first year, growing to profits of $3.4 million in the fifth year. Cash flow was far in excess of operating needs. If these projections are correct, then the company should be the lender and not the borrower. What typically happens is there is a great need to demonstrate a company will be successful, so aggressive assumptions on sales units and pricing are incorporated, such that they obliterate the need for any funding needs.

As previously stated, an excellent source for checking the reality of your financial results relative to industry information is *Annual Statement Studies: Financial Ratio Benchmarks*, prepared by the Risk Management Association. This publication is not free, but hopefully you can find it in a business library or at an organization that focuses on small business. The information is presented in NAICS detail. North American Industry Classification System is the standard used by the federal government for classifying business establishments for the purpose of collecting, analyzing, and publishing statistical data related to the U.S. business economy. NAICS was developed in 1997 to replace the Standard Industrial Classification (SIC) system), so it is very granular.

As part of your reality check, you should conduct a sensitivity or stress test on your projected financial results. You need to do this since your banker and/or angel funder will conduct this analysis as part of their due diligence. To do this, you take the key assumptions, individually and collectively, and calculate the financial outcomes if lower results are obtained (for example, if sales are only 50 percent of forecast, the big contract is six months delayed, manufacturing costs are 150 percent of the forecast, interest rates double, etc.).

REFERENCE MATERIALS

Books and references for better understanding basic financial, accounting, and record-keeping concepts include those noted below. Try visiting college or community college bookstores and looking for their basic accounting texts, which you may be able to buy used. A visit to an online bookseller like Amazon.com is also suggested.

- *Accounting Demystified*, by Leita A. Hart

- *Accounting for Non-Accountants*, by Dr. Wayne A. Label

- *Essentials of Accounting*, by Leslie K. Breitner and Robert N. Anthony

- *Financial and Managerial Accounting*, by Charles T. Horngren, Walter T. Harrison Jr., and M. Suzanne Oliver

Key Lessons

- ✓ The financial section incorporates information from all the previous sections and converts it to a common language—money.

- ✓ A small business, especially a start-up, should focus on cash flow and not income.

- ✓ Spell out your key assumptions in plain English.

- ✓ Determine whether to use cash or accrual accounting.

- ✓ Reality test your projected financial results.

- ✓ Make sure financial information displayed in this section is in sync with financial information shown in all other sections, including the executive summary. The amount of funding requested from a bank or angel investor should be supported with information contained in the financial statements.

- ✓ Use only a few financial ratios, if any, in your business plan and make sure you know the story they tell.

Note: If your financial statements are too large to include in these spaces, print them out and put them in a folder.

List your assumptions from which the three financial statements will be constructed.

Prepare your income statement, cash flow statement, and balance sheet.

Prepare your statement of start-up expenditures.

In a comparison of your results with industry norms, are there major differences? If yes, note the reasons.

Chapter 14

JUST IN CASE

*What You Should Include
in Your Appendix*

Think About It

Does my appendix...

✓ Include material that is of interest and importance but is not
germane to the key message?

✓ Contain too much information, which makes the business plan
too bulky?

Think about if you want or need to have an appendix. The
case for an appendix is it moves details to the back and thus focuses
the reader on the big picture and key messages in the individual
sections. The case against an appendix is it tends to "bulk up" the
whole business plan, which may give the appearance of a document
too big to get into. There is no right or wrong answer to have or not

have an appendix, but of the hundreds of business plans I have been involved with, very few have had an appendix.

If you have an appendix, it will be like your file cabinet. You will probably be the only one who knows the material is in there. Regardless, the material placed in an appendix should be as "readable" as the material in the front portion of your business plan, and it should be well organized. Include photos, detailed resumes, brochures, floor plans and layouts, technical drawings, patents, and any other documents that would overly bulk up the main sections of the plan and make it difficult reading. Some entrepreneurs include the detailed monthly financial statements in the appendix, choosing to have only the annual information in the finance section, so they can focus on the big picture.

Often bankers will request copies of tax returns, your personal net worth statement, and any outstanding loan agreements. As these involve personal information, I would not include them in the business plan but as a separate submission to the bank.

Chapter 15

PASSION TIME

Business Planning for Nonprofits

Most of what has been discussed up to this point applies directly to nonprofits. A common axiom is that nonprofits should be run like a for-profit business. While this is generally true, there are some unique structural aspects of a nonprofit that must be considered, and these should be included in your business plan. To start a small business, you need passion. To start a nonprofit, you need a double dose of passion. However, your passion needs to be focused for a specific purpose, or your start-up nonprofit may get stretched too thin, especially at the outset.

You need a business plan for the start-up or expansion of a nonprofit for all the same reasons you do for a for-profit enterprise. But additionally, you need to make the case for your mission, explain why donors and grantors should provide funding, and seek a qualified board of directors (sometimes called board of trustees). In fact, since a nonprofit business plan contains more information about mission and vision, it is commonly referred to as a strategic plan.

A THREE-STEP PROCESS

Unlike forming an LLC or other for-profit company where there is typically one application needed to set up your legal structure, to form a nonprofit, it takes three. You first apply to a state to become a corporation under its Non-Profit Corporation Act, then you apply to the IRS for federal tax-exempt status, and finally back to the state with IRS certification in hand to obtain state income tax-exempt status. With these certifications, not only will you not have to pay federal and state income taxes, but donations to your nonprofit are tax deductible to the givers.

As part of the IRS filing, you will need to describe your intended activities and demonstrate why they should be considered for nonprofit status. There are many forms of nonprofits to apply for, from 501(c) 1 through 28 (these numbers refer to sections of the IRS tax code), and it often takes about six months between obtaining your state incorporation certificate and your IRS federal tax exempt clearance. During this time, as you are seeking funding from donors, you are in the position of stating your nonprofit status as pending. While there is some probability your application will be rejected, if you have been thorough in your application, there should be a very low chance of this happening. Thus, do not plan on spending a lot of money at the outset since donations may be slow in arriving as some donors may want to wait until you have the tax-exempt papers in hand.

Do you have a "pure" nonprofit idea or one that is a mix of nonprofit and for-profit activities? If the latter case is your situation, then you probably need two separate companies—one for each part of the overall business. For example, AARP (American Association of Retired Persons) has both a for-profit business for selling insurance and products and a nonprofit business for being an advocate for people over 50.

MARKETING AND DEVELOPMENT

In a nonprofit strategic plan, the marketing plan is expanded to a marketing and development plan. Marketing addresses the nonprofit's target market—your potential clients. Review Chapter 10 on how to identify, target, and reach this group.

Nonprofits also have a second set of customers—those individuals or entities who will be making contributions or volunteering their time and/or services. Nonprofits usually call this fund-raising and friend-raising development. In your strategic plan, there should be a separate section addressing how you will achieve funding levels to support your efforts to carry out your mission.

When creating the development plan, you should be mindful of the metrics used to describe activities and success. Unlike most for-profit companies where success is measured in monetary terms, in a nonprofit, financial success is achieved if you have sufficient financial resources to carry out your mission. For other success metrics, most nonprofit organizations collect much information about the "inputs"—how many resources like staffing, volunteers, purchases, machines, and number of offices were used to achieve the results. They also collect a good deal of information about the "outputs"—how many items were made and sold, reports prepared, patients seen, speeches given, and so forth. But for a nonprofit, what warms the hearts and minds of potential donors are the "outcomes." If the non-profit is a medical clinic, examples of outcomes would be how many lives were saved, how many families were kept intact, and how many days were not lost at work. Inputs and outputs usually are gathered from the organization's accounting system or other readily collected data. Outcomes usually belong to the customer—the people or organizations the nonprofit is helping—and are often only available by survey. For this reason, you should take the opportunity and define what success means to your nonprofit before customers, donors, the press, or others do it for you.

GOVERNANCE

As a corporation, a nonprofit must have a board of directors, board officers, and bylaws. For help with writing your bylaws, each state has a statute, often called the "nonprofit corporation act," which sets the minimum governance requirements, such as the number of board members, board member eligibility, number and title of board and management officers, meeting frequency, meeting locations, and reporting requirements. These are the minimums, and you should edit/expand your bylaws to meet these requirements. You might consider having board committees, such as finance/audit, nominating, development, compensation, and/or executive; as well as director term limits and deciding if all directors will be required to make personal contributions, etc.

Board Member Best Practices

Board members need to recognize that the nonprofit belongs to the public and the board is planning and conducting oversight of the nonprofit's activities on behalf of the public. In your deliberations while creating the board, you should consider the pros and cons of having a large board with a focus on fund-raising or a smaller board focused on governance. It is not as black and white as this wording might suggest. With a large board, it is difficult for all to feel engaged, so what usually happens is a powerful executive committee is created and, in effect, there is a two-tier board structure. A smaller board is easier to manage and have each member feel engaged, but you will need to find other mechanisms for fund-raising. It is usually the case that board members are all volunteers who have no salary but get reimbursed for reasonable expenses. However, if they are very supportive of the mission, they often forgo the reimbursements.

IT'S LIKE THIS: A city symphony orchestra decided it was important that its board be focused on fund-raising and established a 50-person board and selected board members who had the personal or employer-supported ability to make sizeable annual financial contributions. They found it difficult to assemble all 50 board members at once and discuss the governance, oversight responsibilities, and activities of the board, so they formed a 10-person executive committee. At board meetings, when an item subject to board vote was raised, it was prefaced with the comment that the executive committee has already reviewed and approved it. The implication to the other 40 board members was clear: Just rubber stamp the vote—all we want is your money. For some, this was OK, but for others, it was unacceptable as each of the 50 board members has an equal fiduciary responsibility, so they resigned.

As mentioned previously and here again for emphasis, many states forbid paid nonprofit staff from being voting board members. Even where this is not prohibited, it is not a good board governance practice to have paid staff as voting board members. This means the founders who continue on as paid staff while attending and participating in board meetings cannot vote on key items and will have the board consider their performance evaluation, compensation, and tenure in executive session (in other words, without the founders/officers in the room).

Another best practice is not contracting with board member companies to carry out nonprofit business, as there is opportunity for conflicts of interest, and one of a nonprofit's most important assets is its reputation. In the few cases where a board member's firm is uniquely qualified for the contract, hold a discussion with that board member not in the room and require board approval.

Form 990 Activities Report

Since a nonprofit is serving some type of public good and contributions usually qualify for tax preference, the results of the nonprofit become part of the public record and are available on various websites. Each year, using Form 990, nonprofits must report their activities, including the salaries of key staff and the names of all donors who give more than $5,000.

Many donors use Form 990 to find out how much of their contributions go to the nonprofit's programs and how much is absorbed by fund-raising efforts and administrative costs (for example, administrative salaries). However, if you have a very small nonprofit, you can file your Form 990 without this information (most small tax-exempt organizations with gross receipts normally $50,000 or less qualify).

What for many years was purely a financial report, Form 990 has become a corporate governance best practices report with yes/no questions regarding such matters as having a whistleblower policy, sharing the Form 990 report with the board before filing with the IRS, using an independent salary survey in determining CEO/ executive director compensation, and having a formal records retention policy.

Since on Form 990 you will be reporting the allocation of your contributions and expenses to your programs, fund-raising efforts, and administration, you will want to design your organization and activities to show favorable results—meaning, your nonprofit is focused on the people you serve and not on your compensation and benefits. You will also need an accounting system that collects and reports information that can be placed in this format.

FINANCIAL REPORTING FOR NONPROFITS

Much of the information in the chapter on financial statements applies equally to nonprofits; the key differences are in the layout and names of the financial statements. First, what we referred to as the balance sheet becomes the statement of financial position. In addition, since a nonprofit has no stockholders or investors, upon dissolving a nonprofit, any remaining assets must be rolled over to another nonprofit (or local or state government) rather than going to the founders or subsequent participants. Hence, the stockholders' equity section becomes the net assets section. The net assets section has three components capturing the nature of any donations classified as "unrestricted," "temporarily restricted," or "permanently restricted." (*Note:* The U.S. accounting regulator, the Financial Accounting Standards Board, has issued a ruling that will change this three-category description of donations and make it two. This and other nonprofit accounting practice changes will become effective for fiscal years beginning after December 15, 2017.)

There are several nuances in accounting rules and conventions between for-profits and nonprofits, which your accountant can help you with. You should seek an accountant with nonprofit experience and other nonprofit clients.

Here is a visual comparison of for-profit and nonprofit financial statements:

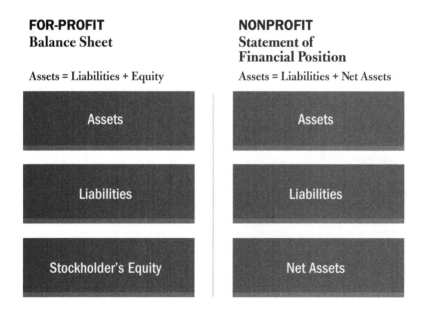

FOR-PROFIT
Balance Sheet

Assets = Liabilities + Equity

Assets

Liabilities

Stockholder's Equity

NONPROFIT
Statement of Financial Position

Assets = Liabilities + Net Assets

Assets

Liabilities

Net Assets

Since the purpose of a nonprofit is mission and not income, the bottom line of the statement of financial position is net assets rather than income, like it is for a for-profit company. Thus, the for-profit's income statement becomes a statement of activities for nonprofits.

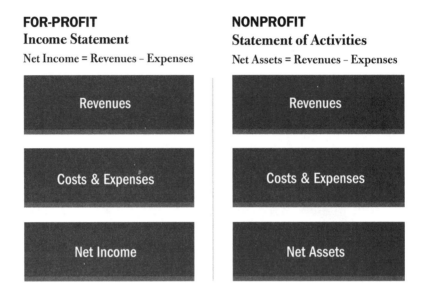

FOR-PROFIT
Income Statement
Net Income = Revenues – Expenses

Revenues

Costs & Expenses

Net Income

NONPROFIT
Statement of Activities
Net Assets = Revenues – Expenses

Revenues

Costs & Expenses

Net Assets

NONPROFIT OR FOR-PROFIT?

Some entrepreneurs question if they should form a for-profit or non-profit entity. If your mission qualifies for nonprofit status and you have the passion to make a contribution to the community, the decision comes down to two criteria.

First is how the company will generate revenues. If you are dependent on grants and having donors make contributions that are tax deductible, then you should be a nonprofit. However, if you are able to sell your product or service at a price that will generate an acceptable rate of return, then you should form a for-profit company.

Second are your personal goals for creating "wealth." As the founder of the nonprofit, you can also be an employee earning a salary and a wide range of benefits, such as health care insurance, savings plan, and vacation/holiday/sick days. However, since the nonprofit is funded with tax-exempt donations/grants to serve a public purpose, when you leave/retire you cannot take any assets with you. Similarly, if the nonprofit closes down, its assets must be transferred to another nonprofit or government entity. Compare this to a for-profit company, where the assets of the company belong to the owners and owners can sell their investments at any time.

In a nonprofit, contributions to the community are made by the company, while in a for-profit, the company and the owners can make charitable contributions. Two widely known examples are Warren Buffett at Berkshire Hathaway and Bill Gates at Microsoft who started and ran very successful companies, then took their investments, formed foundations, and made personal charitable contributions.

ONLINE RESOURCES

There is a wealth of information online for planning a nonprofit. Following are just a few resources:

- SCORE has a nonprofit planning guide you can download for free at www.score.org/search/site/nonprofitplanningguide.

- The IRS website has a section focused on topics for nonprofits and charities: www.irs.gov/charities-non-profits

- BoardSource (www.boardsource.org) provides training, education, and a wealth of information about nonprofit best practices. Two of their many books especially worth reading are *Ten Basic Responsibilities of Nonprofit Boards*, by Richard T. Ingram, and *The Nonprofit Board Answer Book: A Practical Guide for Board Members and Chief Executives*, by BoardSource.

- For the blue ribbon review and analysis of nonprofit best governance practices, refer to the American Red Cross, 2006 exhaustive review of best practices. You can view the 162-page report at www.redcross.org/images/MEDIA_CustomProductCatalog/ m4240145_BOGGovernanceReport.pdf.

- Check out Guide Star (guidestar.org) for more information about Form 990. This nonprofit organization gathers and publicizes information about other nonprofit organizations.

Key Lessons

✓ Establishing a nonprofit is a three-step application and approval process and can take as long as six months to complete.

✓ A nonprofit is a corporation with all the same governance and reporting issues as a for-profit business, in addition to having a board of directors on which paid employees usually cannot be voting members.

✓ Whether to set up your company as a nonprofit or for-profit entity depends on your funding sources and your personal financial goals.

Describe the following information for your nonprofit. For the financial statements and development plan, which are multipage documents, print separately and keep in a separate folder.

Mission Statement	
Developmental Plan	
Potential Board Members	
Financial Statements	

FINANCING 101

At the outset of this book, we noted a business plan is written primarily for yourself—to help you decide whether or not to start or grow a business, to set goals and benchmarks, and to use the process for developing a set of compelling and consistent messages describing your business and why you will be successful.

We also noted that other important readers of your business plan are potential funders. In this section, we discuss the funding of your business idea. Through an appreciation of how these funding sources are structured, you may modify your business plan or its messages so it has the best chance of being funded.

To provide a bridge between developing the business idea with all its components—the business plan—and applying for and receiving the necessary funding, consider the following process, which is ongoing through the life of your business:

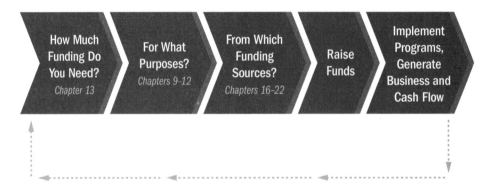

For the past 15 chapters, we have focused on designing your business and determining the resources needed to make it successful, both pre-start-up and ongoing. From this, we developed the financial forecasts.

Section III focuses on the third element in the above diagram: determining the best funding sources. Following is an overview of the many funding sources that will be covered in the next several chapters:

	NONDILUTIVE		DILUTIVE
INTERNAL	**Business (Chapter 16)**		
	▪ Revenues ▪ Own Sweat Equity	▪ Payments Terms	▪ Team's Sweat Equity
	Personal (Chapter 17)		
	▪ Life Savings ▪ Sale of Assets	▪ Home Equity ▪ Credit Cards	
EXTERNAL	**Third Parties**		
	Grants (Chapter 18)	Debt	Equity
	▪ SBIR ▪ Economic Development ▪ Donation and Reward-Type Crowdfunding ▪ Nonprofit Grants and Donations	▪ Bank Loans, w/wo SBA guarantee (Chapter 19) ▪ Company Credit Cards (Chapter 20) ▪ Family and Friends (Chapter 20) ▪ Peer-to-Peer Crowdfunding (Chapter 20) ▪ Leasing and Factoring (Chapter 20)	▪ Family and Friends (Chapter 20) ▪ Equity Crowdfunding (Chapter 21) ▪ Angel Investors (Chapter 22) ▪ Venture Capital (Chapter 22)

Adapted from Elizabeth Edwards' book, *Startup: The Complete Handbook for Launching a Company for Less*

Note how the chart is organized. From top to bottom are internal funding sources the business generates itself (which pertain to those already in business), personal sources, and finally external sources. On the left are sources in which you do not give up/sell equity/ownership in the business. These are called nondilutive sources. On the right are funding alternatives in which you "trade" funding for an ownership interest in the company, in other words, diluted sources. There are no right or wrong options; it is finding the right fit for your situation.

Finally, below are statistics of actual start-up funding by source. You might start to think a big bank loan or a large angel investment is the way to go. But as you can see in the chart 95 percent of funding for start-ups comes from your personal funds and family and friends. In my experience, for companies to get to the stage where they are ready for angel funding, they need to have a product/service, some market traction, and revenue to validate the business model. To obtain these milestones, they will have invested at least $50,000 and maybe as high as $500,000 from personal funds and family and friends.

Getting Started

Younger firms have relied more on personal savings or credit-card borrowing to start or buy a business, rather than traditional bank lending, according to 2014 Census data.[1]

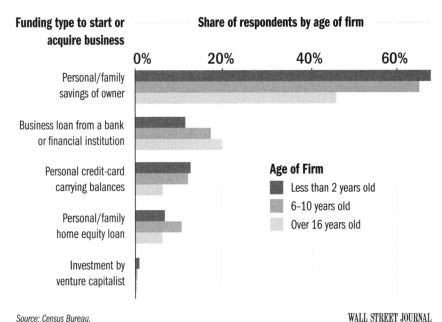

Funding type to start or acquire business

Share of respondents by age of firm

- Personal/family savings of owner
- Business loan from a bank or financial institution
- Personal credit-card carrying balances
- Personal/family home equity loan
- Investment by venture capitalist

Age of Firm
- Less than 2 years old
- 6–10 years old
- Over 16 years old

Source: Census Bureau, 2014 Annual Survey of Entrepreneurs

WALL STREET JOURNAL
"Funding Sources Shift for Startups: Young Firms Move Toward Savings, Credit Cards and Away from Bank Loans, Home Equity," by Ruth Simon and Paul Overberg

While I discuss all the financing listed in the funding sources chart in this section, the chapters addressing bank lending, angel financing, and crowdfunding are the longest because I find clients need these insights.

---

[1] An obvious omission from the table on page 184 is crowdfunding because it is relatively new and the industry statistics are not cleanly broken down by type (e.g., donations, rewards, peer to peer, equity, and real estate) or geography. According to research conducted by Krista Tuomi of American University, worldwide, it is estimated that $1.1 billion was raised in equity crowdfunding in 2014 (compared with $11.08 billion in peer-to-peer lending, and $6.1 billion in other forms of crowdfunding). That's small in comparison to $24 billion in angel investments.

Chapter 16

THE INSIDE TRACK

Funding from Internal Sources

A business that generates more cash than it needs to spend is one measure of success. You can decide to use these "extra" funds to pay yourself a dividend, pay off debts, create a "rainy day fund," or start new projects to grow your business. These "extra" funds might be ongoing and predicable. In addition, in an established business, there are often one-time opportunities to generate cash.

Revenues

Revenues are the lifeblood of any company. As long as your revenues exceed your costs, you have positive cash flow and can use these funds for new initiatives. It is helpful if your revenues come in before your costs are due. For example, major oil companies receive payment for gasoline sold at the pump right away, but pay for the crude oil about 90 days after receipt. On a much smaller scale, you might be able to sell a service before you must pay consultants or wait to rent equipment until a contract is signed. In each case, you are operating on the "float."

Payment Terms

You have two sets of payment terms—when customers pay you and when you pay your vendors. Standard terms are payment is due within 30 days from billing. To speed up cash flow, some companies offer a discount, like 1 percent for payment within 10 days. While you will set your customers' payment terms relative to your cash flow needs, you need to be aware of industry practice so you do not lose customers by not being competitive.

On the other side, you pay invoices. Consider asking vendors for more favorable credit terms, especially if you are a long-term, good paying customer. If you have multiple suppliers, use the ones with the best terms. In very tight times, you can slow down payments for both invoices and credit card balances, but you run the risk of being cut off from future business and negatively impacting your credit scores and D&B ratings.

Sweat Equity

As the founder, in tight times, you can decide to take less salary or none, and use these funds to finance new projects. If you have a team, you can ask them to also take less salary, but you will probably have to give them something in exchange. Often this in the form of stock options or another form of equity. That is why this funding alternative is in the dilutive column.

Key Lessons

✓ A successful business generates cash in excess of current needs, which can be used for many purposes, including reinvesting in the business to facilitate growth.

✓ Payment terms can be adjusted to generate cash flow, but it is usually a one-shot opportunity.

✓ You and staff can take lower pay and use the freed-up cash to fund needed projects.

How much cash do I currently have?

_____

_____

If no other sources are used, how much cash do I need?

_____

_____

How much cash can I generate from these business sources, and of this, how much is available for new projects?

SOURCES	TOTAL $ RAISED	AMOUNT AVAILABLE FOR NEW PROJECTS
Revenues		
Changing Customer Payment Terms		
Changing Your Payment Terms to Vendors		
Reducing Your and Team's Salary		
TOTAL		

Chapter 17

PRIVATE RESERVE

Funding from Personal Sources

Most start-ups get initial funding from the founder(s) as a show of good faith to gain commitments from financiers. Also, later funders want to make sure the founders believe in their business idea, which is demonstrated with the first funding because it is the most risky.

Life Savings

This can be in the form of bank accounts, stocks, and bonds; but typically is in the form of IRAs, and other retirement accounts. All these can be used to fund your business.

If you go to a franchise expo, you will most surely see a few booths staffed with salespeople happy to share with you how to use your 401(k) or other pension/savings plan to fund your franchise or business start-up. Their argument is that these might be the only funds available, you created the funds to be used at a subsequent time, and if you are truly supportive and confident of your own ideas, why not use these funds? There may be some truth to this sale pitch, but think carefully about using these saved funds for an idea that may not work. If the business is not successful, what funds do you have for your retirement years—how can these retirement funds be replaced?

Sale of Assets

Maybe you own a vacation home or a boat, have stored away a stamp collection given to you by your grandfather, or have a portfolio of stocks and bonds. These can be sold to fund your business idea. When thinking of the value these assets can contribute to your business, remember that you will pay tax on any gains, so think in terms of after-tax amounts.

Home Equity Loans

While it takes an external party like a bank to create a home equity loan, since it is a personal asset your already own, I have listed it here.

If you own a house or other property in which there is equity, you can get a home equity loan. In essence, you will be transferring equity from your personal to your business account. With the high failure rate of start-up businesses, some people prefer to keep their personal and business funds separate. It becomes a question of how much money is needed; how much, if not all, will you draw down from your accounts; how many alternative funding sources are available; how serious you are about your business idea; and most important, how much risk you are prepared to take on.

Regardless of what happens to the business, if you take a home equity loan, you have the obligation to repay it, or risk losing your home. And if you own the house jointly with a spouse or another person, you will need their approval for the home equity loan.

Credit Cards

Many of us have a wallet with several credit cards. To generate some quick cash, you can charge items to the cards and not pay the card balance when it is due. Of course, you can only use the card up to its credit limit and overdue payments will impact your credit score. Additionally, the interest rate on credit card overdue balances can be about 18 percent, which might be higher than other alternatives. Of all the funding options, this is the easiest as you do not have to involve others—just do it.

Key Lessons

- ✓ Use personal assets to initially fund your business idea.

- ✓ As a sign of accomplishment, get the business off the ground before asking others, including family and friends, to provide funding assistance.

- ✓ Evaluate the benefits and risks of transferring funds from personal savings/retirement and home equity accounts to your business account.

Have I thought through the risks and benefits of using a retirement account or my home's equity to fund my business idea?

How much cash can I generate from personal resources?

SOURCES	$
Life Savings	
Sale of Assets (List Each)	
Home Equity Loans	
Credit Cards	
TOTAL	

Chapter 18

"FREE" MONEY

*Funding from External Sources—
Grants and Donations*

In this first of three chapters addressing external funding
sources, we review grants and donations. As the name implies, this is
"free" money. It does not need to be paid back and you do not have
to provide equity in your company in exchange. However, while the
money is "free," it is not without obligation. To obtain the funds, there
is usually an application process. Then, once the funds are received,
you usually must report to the grantor and demonstrate that the funds
are being used for the intended and agreed-upon purposes.

Individuals and for-profit companies generally do not provide grants
to for-profits, since they do not receive a charitable tax deduction, get
equity in the company, or have a loan that gets paid back with interest. A few for-profit, special-purpose government grants are noted
below. For-profit general government grants are problematic, since
the government uses tax dollars, and if you open a coffee shop with
a federal grant, your competitor down the block will rightfully com-
plain that her tax dollars are being used to create direct competition.

Small Business Innovation Research (SBIR)

These grants are provided by government agencies, so if you are considering them as a funding source, you should include establishing relationships with applicable federal agencies in your business plan. From the SBIR website (www.sbir.gov):

> The Small Business Innovation Research program is a highly competitive program that encourages domestic small businesses to engage in Federal Research/Research and Development (R/R&D) that has the potential for commercialization. Through a competitive awards-based program, SBIR enables small businesses to explore their technological potential and provides the incentive to profit from its commercialization. By including qualified small businesses in the nation's R&D arena, high-tech innovation is stimulated, and the United States gains entrepreneurial spirit as it meets its specific research and development needs.

The SBIR website lists 12 federal agencies, with each administering its own program within guidelines established by Congress. These agencies specify research projects/ideas in their requests for bids and accept proposals from small businesses. Awards are made on a competitive basis after proposal evaluation.

The SBIR Program is structured in three phases:

- **Phase I:** The objective of Phase I is to establish the technical merit, feasibility, and commercial potential of the proposed R/R&D efforts and to determine the ability of the company to produce the goods/services/research in a quality manner prior to providing further federal support in Phase II. SBIR Phase I awards are normally a maximum of $150,000 for six months.

- **Phase II:** The objective of Phase II is to continue the R/R&D efforts initiated in Phase I. Funding is based on the results achieved in Phase I, in addition to the scientific and technical merit and commercial potential of the project proposed in Phase II. Only Phase I awardees are eligible for a Phase II award. Phase II awards normally do not exceed $1 million for two years.

- **Phase III:** The objective of Phase III is for the small business to pursue commercialization objectives resulting from the Phase I/II R/R&D activities. The SBIR program does not fund Phase III. Some federal agencies, however, may fund R&D or production contracts for products, processes, or services intended for use by the U.S. government.

Economic Development

Many states and counties offer incentives to locate or grow a business in their area. Their mission is to create new businesses and jobs. There is also one federal program with the same objectives.

- **HUBZone:** This is a Small Business Administration (SBA) program for small companies that operate and employ people in Historically Underutilized Business Zones. Refer to the SBA website (www.sba.gov) for a full description of the program and maps where these areas are located to see if you qualify. The benefits of qualifying for HUBZone status include competitive and sole-source contracting, 10 percent price evaluation preference in open contract competitions (whereby you can be up to 10 percent over the low bid and still win the contract), and subcontracting opportunities.

- **County and State Economic Development:** This program is usually targeted to employment and new business formation. New businesses can be start-ups or transfers from other areas, but in both situations, the result is new-job creation. Grant funds can be used to support capital expenditures, such as buildings, equipment, and even software development. While there might be some incentives, such as low interest rates and length of time to repay, there may be obligations to repay the funds. To foster new businesses, many counties run business plan competitions, and these usually result in true grants to the winners.

Donation and Reward Crowdfunding

Three years ago, crowdfunding was mostly known for reward platforms like Kickstarter and Indiegogo. Now, crowdfunding is a general platform supporting many different types of participation, including donations, rewards, peer-to-peer lending (see Chapter 20), equity (see Chapter 21), and real estate. In this chapter, we focus on reward platforms, which in exchange for offering a gift or product result in funds that do not have to be paid back. Later, in the "Financing Roundup" and "Show of Hands" chapters, we will cover debt and equity crowdfunding, respectively.

Crowdfunding describes the network and pooled money available, usually via the internet, to support entrepreneurial efforts. Crowdfunding occurs for a variety of purposes, including disaster relief, citizen journalism, artists seeking support from fans, political campaigns, funding a start-up company or movie, creating free software, scientific research, and more. Search online, and you will find more than 125 crowdfunding sites in the United States.

There is a downside to crowdfunding—the protection of intellectual property rights, since once posted, your idea is ripe for being copied or stolen. Thus, this type of funding is better for companies that have a competitive advantage secured by trade secrets or strong patents, not businesses in which success depends on being first to market with an easily copied process or service.

Kickstarter (www.kickstarter.com) was one of the first crowdfunding sites. Its approach is to facilitate the gathering of monetary resources from the general public, a model that avoids traditional investment avenues. People apply to Kickstarter to have a project posted on the site, and Kickstarter provides guidelines on what types of projects will be accepted. Project owners choose a deadline and a target minimum of funds to raise. If the target is not reached by the deadline, no funds are collected. Money pledged by donors is collected using Amazon Payments (https://payments.amazon.com/sdui/sdui/index.htm).

Kickstarter takes 5 percent of the funds raised; Amazon charges an additional 3 to 5 percent. Thus, you will receive about 91 percent of the funds raised. Unlike many venues for fund-raising or investment, Kickstarter claims no ownership over the projects and the work they produce. However, projects launched on the site are permanently archived and accessible to the public. After funding is completed, projects and uploaded media cannot be edited or removed from the site.

There is no guarantee that people who post projects on Kickstarter will deliver on their projects or use the money to implement them, or that the completed projects will meet backers' expectations. In fact, Kickstarter has been accused of providing little quality control. Kickstarter advises sponsors to use their own judgment in supporting a project. They also warn project leaders that they could be liable for legal damages from sponsors for failure to deliver on promises. For example, in May 2011, a film student raised $1,726 to make a film but plagiarized another film instead. The student publicly apologized, and the issue has since been settled. Projects can also fail even after funds have been successfully raised, when creators underestimate the total costs required or the technical difficulties to be overcome.

Is your start-up prime for crowdfunding? An article by AJ Kumar for the Young Entrepreneur Council[1] listed five reasons your start-up may not be ready for crowdfunding:

1. You can't offer a discrete product (usually a tangible consumer product).

2. You haven't thoroughly defined your distribution channels (this includes packaging and shipping).

---

[1] http://venturebeat.com/2012/07/28/5-reasons-your-start-up-isnt-ready-for-crowdfunding

3. Your prototypes aren't effective (need a close-to-market product rather than one in testing).

4. You can't commit time to customer service (crowdfunding brings many small customers/investors who need attention).

5. You aren't prepared for overfunding (what will you do with more funds than originally targeted—just putting the money in the bank is not acceptable to investors).

Reward types of crowdfunding work best when there is a tangible product that investors hope to receive in the future. Idea businesses like consulting, and charities are much more difficult undertakings. Not addressed here are the donation-type crowdfunding platforms, which are used to raise funds for personal rather than business purposes.

Nonprofit Grants and Donations

Much of this in covered in the chapter on nonprofits.

A good source for finding federal government-sourced grants is www.grants.gov.

Key Lessons

✓ There are few grants to for-profit businesses.

✓ Donation and reward crowdfunding platforms continue to grow and be a source of funding to start a business.

✓ States and counties have economic development initiatives to facilitate new businesses and job creation.

Which grant opportunities fit with my business, and of these, what is the range of funding amounts that are typically available?

Does a donation/reward type of crowdfunding campaign fit my business, and do I have the network to generate sufficient leads to fund my plan? Which crowdfunding platforms will I explore?

Chapter 19

BANK ON IT

Funding from External Sources—
Banks and SBA Loans

This chapter title uses the word "bank" as a reference for all the institutions that lend money for a specified period of time and charge interest. The lender receives his profit from interest paid, according to an agreed upon schedule and, of course, the repayment of the principal amount borrowed. Loans can be provided by many sources, including national, regional, and community banks, credit unions, micro lenders, financing companies, financing arms of equipment manufacturers, investment banks, and more. In some cases, angel investors will provide loans as a bridge to equity funding (angels are discussed in Chapter 22, "Heavenly Financing"). This chapter focuses primarily on commercial banks because the processes and characteristics are similar for all lenders.

BANK LOANS

When you take out a loan, the bank becomes your "partner" with the common goal of making the business a success. The bank's position is mostly passive, especially if you make all payments on time and maintain a periodic communication with your bank's small business loan officer on your progress.

As bank lending is the most common source of loans, the following discussion provides a general outline of the commercial bank loan process to start up small businesses. Each bank has its own processes, market niches, and loan portfolio; therefore, this is a summary of common practices and does not describe any one bank.

Set Up a Meeting with a Loan Officer

The first thing you need to do if you want a small business loan is to meet with a small business loan officer. But before making an appointment, visit the bank's website to see what they say about small business lending. Making an appointment, rather than walking in, demonstrates that you are a serious applicant and ensures the appropriate bank officer will be present.

How do you find out who is the best person to contact and which banks to approach? A good resource to start with is the SBA. Each SBA district office maintains a list, often posted on their website, of all the banks in the area that participate in SBA-loan programs as well as the number of loans and the value of the loans made each month. While the SBA-loan programs would be a small portion of a bank's overall loan portfolio, they are a good representation of which area banks are interested in the small business loan market. At the SBA, SCORE, SBDCs, and Women's Business Centers, there is a booklet published by the SBA called *Small Business Resource*, which lists banks per area with small business loan officer contact information. Another approach would be to go to the bank's district office.

One approach that has been successful is to take no written materials to the first session, but relate to the loan officer the type of business you are considering starting or the business you are growing as well as the amount of funding you are looking for, and then asking if the bank is interested in this opportunity and what information they would like you to come back with. This will assist you in determining which banks have the most interest and will help in shaping your application and targeting your business plan.

Alternatively, call the small business loan officer at the bank(s) where you currently have your personal and/or business accounts, because these banks know your character, client history, and your financial behaviors, and thus they can reduce the uncertainty, which is the primary reason for a loan decline. On this call, ask what would be beneficial to discuss in a first face-to-face meeting and request that the bank prepare a checklist of financial documents they require.

Only need funds for a truck or car? Consider a leasing program to get the business started and then, after generating cash flow and building a track record, convert to a conventional loan. A lease can be obtained from a bank, leasing company, or dealer.

If you are uncomfortable discussing financial matters and/or think it may be better to have two people present, then bring someone else along. Bringing your accountant, for example, demonstrates you are serious about your business.

Documents to Bring to Your Meeting

You scheduled your meeting with the loan officer. Now you need to make sure you are prepared for the meeting by bringing the right documents with you. Following is a list of what you should bring, which, in essence, help "prove you are worth the money":

- Business plan, including assumptions and financial forecasts for a least three years into the future

- Three years of financial statements (income statement, cash flow statement, and balance sheet) prepared by your accountant and signed by you. If the statements are prepared using the cash basis, restate using accrual accounting.

- Your business and personal tax returns for the past three years, including all schedules. Bring three years of each, if available.

- Your personal net worth statement with details of any assets that can be used as collateral (for example, house, car, savings account), including any joint assets with your spouse

- Written documentation of how much money you will invest in the business, the rationale for the loan size being requested, the purposes for which the funds will be used, and a plan/structure for repaying the loan

- Resume outlining your experience and how it relates to the business you are seeking a loan for

- Details of any loans outstanding

- Any accounts receivable and/or inventory, as it may provide the first level of collateral

- A binder/folder of printouts if you used a computerized record-keeping system, like QuickBooks, so the loan officer can see how serious you are about the business

At the Bank Loan Meeting

The big day has arrived, and you are sitting across from the loan officer. Make sure you are dressed appropriately—first impressions are important. Act and dress the same way you would for a job interview. Have your documents organized in an orderly manner, and have a letter ready for the bank detailing all the materials you are submitting, as well as how appreciative you are of their consideration.

During the meeting, you can expect the loan officer to discuss the bank's process, review your documents, and tell you if any information is missing. Depending on the bank, the loan officer will have loan approval authority or will have to share the information with colleagues on a credit committee. Loan decisions are usually not made at this first meeting.

Criteria Considered in Granting a Loan

How does the bank decide whether to grant your loan, and what criteria do bank officials take into consideration when determining the loan size and terms?

First, a current relationship with the bank is important. If you do not have an account, you should agree to establish one if you are offered a loan. A bank also takes your credit score into account. Know your credit score before going to the bank so you are not surprised and can discuss any shortcomings. Go to www.ftc.gov to order a free credit report.

Conceptually, banks consider themselves to be the fourth or fifth tier of financing. They believe funding first comes from the business, the business owner, the owner's family and friends, investors (angels), home equity loans, and then the bank. However, banks are sensitive to you using all your cash, so it is not necessary to have used up all available funds from these first sources. The goal is to get an appropriate mix of owner- and bank-supplied funding. Generally banks think that of the total funding required, the owners and their sources should invest about 20 percent and the bank 80 percent.

The amount of collateral available is another factor. Best case is collateral equal to the size of the loan plus 25 percent. The bank will make its own calculation of your collateral's value. Remember, the bank does not want to own a used house, car, truck, or manufacturing equipment. Intangible assets, such as bank accounts and investment holdings, may qualify as collateral. Banks will typically require a personal guarantee, which is the business owner's promise that the debt will be paid from personal assets if the business is unable to do so.

Some banks require the business to be cash flow positive at the time of the loan, while others require the applicant to be cash flow positive, considering all funding sources (for example, business, spouse's income, savings accounts). All this is meant to provide comfort that the loan will be repaid. Most banks base decisions on current cash flow rather than projected.

Be aware that some banks are not in the start-up market (but you would already know this from the research you did prior to setting up a meeting, right?). They may make an exception for national franchise operations, but in general, they are only interested in ongoing operations with at least 6 to 12 months' experience. Those that lend to start-ups usually require the owner's house as collateral. Thus, renters have a difficult time getting such loans.

Is It a Yes or a No?

Depending on the bank and loan complexity, the loan review and approval process can take from a few days to a month. After the bank has reviewed your documents and loan application, you will get a response, which could be yes, no, or need more information. If the bank says yes, they will offer a loan with conditions that may be more restrictive than you sought. If you feel the terms are too restrictive, you can provide additional information to hopefully alleviate the bank's concerns, try to negotiate different terms, or if all else fails, walk away and try someplace else. However, if this is the last stop and you need the money, then you will accept the terms if you want your business idea to be implemented. Banks do not like to say no, so they might say loan approval is pending SBA participation. At this point, the bank should volunteer to go to the SBA to request a loan guarantee, but if they do not, ask. The SBA has several programs, and the bank should suggest which one best suits the applicant. The bank may also suggest visiting SCORE, an SBDC, a Women's Business Center, or other resource to obtain assistance with your business plan.

If the bank says no, you should ask the reasons and do it in a manner that is instructive so you can learn from and improve your application. The trend in today's current financial markets is that if the institution you currently bank with says no to your application, it will take visits and applications to three to five other banks before you can get some interest, assuming you have updated your business plan with the suggestions received from the declining bank. Also, if the bank says no, you should ask if it works with "second look" financial institutions. These institutions are often micro-lenders that have less strenuous requirements.

After the Loan Is Granted

Congratulations, your loan has been approved. What can you expect next?

First, be prepared to read and sign many agreements and forms. Banks will also require periodic reporting, detailing how the business is doing and measuring any specific factors in the loan agreement, such as profit margins or reserve balances. This will be required quarterly or annually and includes a narrative, the financial statements prepared by an accountant and signed by the business owner, and personal and business tax returns.

SBA LOAN PROGRAMS

The SBA offers a range of programs, from start-up loans to expansion capital, to facilitate small businesses securing loans from banks and other lending institutions. The SBA itself does not make the loans, but supports, usually through guarantees, the institutions making these loans. Following is an overview of three of the primary loan programs as well as some common myths about SBA loans. For a full explanation of each loan program and a complete list of SBA loans available, visit the SBA website at www.sba.gov.

7(a) Loan Program

The 7(a) Loan Program is the SBA's primary loan program. The SBA reduces risks to lenders by guaranteeing major portions of loans made to small businesses. This enables lenders to offer financing to small businesses they would not otherwise provide. In fiscal year 2015, more than 63,460 7(a) loans were approved. The SBA can guarantee as much as 85 percent on loans of up to $150,000 and 75 percent on larger loans, both with maturities in the 5- to 10-year range. There are several specialized programs within the 7(a) program, and the lender should advise you on which one best fits your needs. Depending on the size of the loan and its term, the SBA upfront guarantee fee that is charged to the lender, but often passed on to the borrower after disbursement, ranges from 0.25 to 3.75 percent. Collateral and personal guarantees are usually required under the 7(a) programs.

504 Loan Program

The 504 Loan Program was designed as an economic development program supporting business expansion and job creation. It provides long-term, fixed-rate subordinate mortgage financing for acquisition and/or renovation of capital assets, including land, buildings, and equipment. In fiscal year 2015, 5,787 loans were approved under the 504 program. Depending on the loan purpose, the maximum amount loaned is $5 million (for the SBA portion) with maturities in the range of 10 to 20 years.

Microloan Program

There are many definitions of what loan size is included in this category. For our purposes, these are any loans up to $50,000, with $10,000 the typical amount. These lenders usually have less stringent requirements than the 7(a) lenders and are used to dealing with borrowers who have less documentation in their business plan.

In the SBA microloan program, funds are provided to specially designated intermediary lenders, which are nonprofit community-based organizations with experience in lending as well as management and technical assistance. These intermediaries administer the microloan program for eligible borrowers and offer loans of up to six years. While interest rates are dependent on many factors, they range from 8 to 13 percent and may require some type of collateral as well as the business owner's personal guarantee. Microloans can be used for working capital, inventory or supplies, furniture or fixtures, and machinery or equipment but may not be used to pay existing debts or to purchase real estate.

SBA Express Loan Program

The SBA offers banks the opportunity to provide business loans in an expedited manner under the SBA Express Loan Program. The bank's paperwork and documentation requirements are reduced so they can provide a loan approval decision with 36 hours. Loans can be for as much as $350,000 for seven years with a negotiated interest rate, which may include a spread of as much as 4.5 to 6.5 percent above the lending rate. However, the SBA only provides up to a 50 percent guarantee for these loans compared with about 85 percent under the 7(a) program.

Veterans Advantage

The Veterans Advantage initiative is a loan program designed for small businesses that are 51 percent or more owned and controlled by veterans; service-disabled veterans; active-duty military service members participating in the military's Transition Assistance Program (TAP); reservists and National Guard members; current spouses of the above; or spouses of service members or veterans who died of a service-connected disability. Loans can be for as much as $5 million, with the upfront SBA-guarantee fee reduced by 50 percent.

SBA LINC

LINC (Leveraging Information and Networks to access Capital) is an online referral tool to connect small business borrowers with participating SBA lenders. Prospective borrowers complete a short online questionnaire. Responses are then forwarded to participating SBA lenders that operate within the small business's county. If lenders are interested in the referral, the lender and prospective borrower's contact information will be exchanged. Completing LINC's online questionnaire does not constitute an actual loan application. Instead, LINC is a tool that small businesses can use to identify potential lenders in their communities.

Loan proceeds can be used for starting a business; working capital; purchasing property, equipment, fixtures or inventory; lease-hold improvements; and refinancing debt.

SBA Loan Myths

There are several common myths about SBA loans and guarantees. Here are three of the most common along with the reality:

1. **The SBA has cash and makes grants and loans directly to applicants.** This is not true. There are grants but in only very specialized situations. Loans are made by commercial banks and other lenders who, in turn, go to the SBA for support. Applicants do not apply directly to the SBA.

2. **SBA programs have a preference for women and minority-owned businesses.** Again, this is not true. All SBA programs are equally available to all small businesses that qualify regardless of business size, character, and financial ability. The one exception is the Veterans Advantage Program (see above) that is provided to businesses owned and controlled by veterans, service-disabled veterans, reservists, or their spouses.

3. To obtain an SBA guarantee, an applicant must have been turned down by three lenders seeking a conventional loan. This is also false. If a bank turns down an applicant for a conventional loan, the bank can go to the SBA if the bank thinks the loan has merit but it does not meet its lending standards.

WILL YOU BE IN THE 10 PERCENT?

What is your banker thinking about as he or she reviews your loan application and business plan?

On the plus side:

- There are 27 million U.S. small businesses with 5 million to 6 million new start-ups each year. Of the total, 6 million have employees and 21 million are run by a sole owner. In other words, starting a small business is a well-tested approach.

- These 27 million small businesses generate more than $9 trillion in revenues, have about $2 trillion in assets, and generate more than 50 percent of the U.S. gross national product. Therefore, there is a cash-generation capacity to pay off a loan in full and on time.

On the negative side:

- About 30 percent of start-ups fail in the first two years and more than half fail in five years. Of the half that are successful, about 10 percent are truly so and 40 percent are marginally so.

- The typical reasons for small business failure are:

  - Owner does not have sufficient experience in the specific business.

  - Owner does not have sufficient experience managing tasks or others.

- Business is undercapitalized either at start-up or at the beginning of a growth spurt.

- Business plan sales forecast was too optimistic—turns out there is not sufficient demand for the company's products and services at the prices needed to generate a profit.

Your small business loan officer has taken all this information into account and is evaluating you and your plan to determine if you will be a successful operation over the term of a loan or if you will fail beforehand. Therefore, your job is to provide convincing evidence first to yourself and then to your banker that your business idea and planning will result in your being in the elite group of 10 percent of all start-ups that are truly successful.

List three banks you plan to approach and the contact information for their small business loan officers.

1.

2.

3.

Review your projected financial statements to ensure they demonstrate your ability to pay periodic (monthly) principal and interest.

What assets can you put up for a fully collateralized loan?

What is your credit score? Will it meet the bank's criteria?

How much capital are you (along with family, friends, and partners) planning to invest? Is it about 20 to 25 percent of the total funding required?

You	
Family	
Friends	

Of the three banks you are planning to approach, what do their websites say about the current lending environment to small businesses and start-up businesses?

1.

2.

3.

Chapter 20

DEBT FINANCING ROUNDUP

Family and Friends, Peer to Peer, and More

In this chapter, we discuss additional sources of financing. These may be sufficient to fund your business idea implementation, or they can be used in conjunction with traditional bank and government funding sources.

Company Credit Card

Issues related to personal and company credit cards are the same. It is easy to stop payment to raise or save cash, but you will incur high interest rates for late payments, and slow payments will reflect poorly on your credit score and D&B rating.

Family and Friends

While buried here on page 217, self-funding augmented with funds from family and friends is the first source of financing. Sometimes just to get started you need to raise funds beyond what you personally can contribute. And often it is necessary to have some "proof of concept" or initial operation before you can approach a bank for debt funding or angels for equity funding. So entrepreneurs turn to family, friends, and acquaintances who believe in the entrepreneur and/or the business idea.

While bank funding is quite formal with much documentation, funding from family and friends tends to be informal. How much information about your business idea to share is always an issue. Usually a very simple business plan is the mechanism for transferring this knowledge. Because of the informality, there is often misunderstanding about what the "deal" is and it is often difficult to have an in-depth conversation. For example, Uncle Fred gives you $25,000, which he thinks is a loan, but you think it is an equity contribution. It is strongly recommended that you have a one-page document signed by both parties describing the nature of the funding and expectations. Especially if it is a loan, both parties need documentation on the interest rate and repayment terms, because the business will take a tax deduction for the interest expense and Uncle Fred will have interest income on which he will need to pay taxes. The IRS sets minimum interest rates that can be used in these situations.

If the funding is considered equity, how many shares or what percentage of the business does Uncle Fred now own and how can he monetize his investment at some point in the future? While it will seem like a lot of paperwork and difficult discussions to have, setting the documentation up front may save relationships with family and friends down the road.

Asheesh Advani has written several books on this subject, which can be found at online booksellers like Amazon.com, including *Business Loans from Family and Friends: How to Ask, Make It Legal & Make It Work.*

Peer to Peer

Earlier, in the grants and donations chapter, we discussed reward crowdfunding, which is offered no-strings-attached. Peer-to-peer (P2P) lending is debt financing, more like a bank loan. However, in a typical bank loan, a single bank provides the full amount of the loan. In P2P lending, particularly via crowdfunding platforms, there are many lenders providing the funds. Examples of P2P lending sites include Lending Tree, Prosper, Funding Circle, and Kiva. Businesses have been slow to embrace P2P lending since many of the crowdfunding sites require a good personal credit score and two years in business. Recently, to gain market share, some sites have reduced these requirements. If you are considering this option, check out the interest rates. I have seen them in the 14 to 19 percent range, which is substantially more than a traditional bank loan or an SBA-guaranteed loan. If you are considering P2P lending, as part of your due diligence in finding the best fit for you, check for consumer complaints against the company.

Working Capital Asset Financing

For companies in business that have inventory and accounts receivable, these are potential sources of short-term financing through intermediaries called factors. These groups purchase your accounts receivables and then handle the collection. They provide funding up front—usually 80 to 90 percent of the A/R value—and the rest (less the factor's commission fee) when the A/R are collected. The higher quality the A/R, the better terms you will achieve. To find factors, contact the International Factoring Association at www.factoring.org.

Leasing

You may reduce your upfront funding requirement by leasing rather than purchasing space. Instead of buying a building, equipment, or vehicle, consider leasing, and, when you have sufficient cash flow, converting the lease to a purchase. While total costs under a lease might be more expensive, up front the monthly expenditures are less than the total purchase price, providing some cash flow flexibility. Often equipment/vehicle companies will have a leasing facility and franchisors will have a lender they refer potential franchisees to.

A lease negotiation has many of the same attributes as a bank loan and thus should not be viewed as a shortcut or reason not to prepare a business plan. The lessor will want to know how you will use the piece of equipment, how you will generate the funds to pay the monthly lease payments and maintain the equipment in reasonable working condition, how the business will generate sufficient funds to eventually buy the equipment, what your personal credit score is, whether a personal guarantee for the lease payments will be required, and what type of collateral you have beyond the piece of equipment.

Contract or Purchase Order Financing

Sometimes you can borrow against a purchase order. The firmer the order and the more creditworthy the customer, the better deal you can negotiate with the lender. While this approach sounds good on paper, it is not a common financing vehicle.

Even when the customer is the U.S. government, there remains questions of your ability to service the contract, the customer's ability to cancel the contract, and, in some cases, the customer's slow payment record.

Key Lessons

- ✓ All funding opportunities should have agreements to document the terms and conditions; it is good practice even if not required.

- ✓ Of those listed in this chapter, family and friends are the most common form of financing, especially for start-ups.

- ✓ Asset-based financing, be it leasing, contract, or working capital, might look attractive, but make sure you know its full cost.

Have I thought through the all the implications of obtaining funds from family and friends? Can I get the appropriate documentation on the nature of their funding?

Which sources will I research, and how much might be available from the best fits?

Chapter 21

A SHOW OF HANDS

Obtaining Equity Crowdfunding

This is the third type of crowdfunding platform. Previously, we discussed donations and rewards, and peer-to-peer lending. Equity crowdfunding can be used by both start-ups and early-stage private companies. Platforms that permit high-net worth individuals (accredited investors) to invest in these businesses have been around for several years. Examples of these platforms are Angel List, Circle Up, and Fundable.

With the U.S. Jobs Act, the Securities and Exchange Commission (SEC) was required to develop a program in which *everyone*, not just high-net-worth individuals, can invest in start-ups, early-stage ventures, and small privately held companies. They did this by October 2015, and it became effective May 16, 2016.

SEC rules now permit most companies to offer and sell securities through crowdfunding. In a gross over-simplification, an entrepreneur can raise up to $1 million in a 12-month period by posting a business plan and equity term sheet (plus audited financial statements if seeking more than $500,000) on an approved website. Accredited investors can provide any amount, but unaccredited investors are limited to between $2,000 and $100,000 in a 12-month period.

In the SEC press release announcing the Regulation Crowdfunding program, Chair Mary Jo White said, "There is a great deal of enthusiasm in the marketplace for crowdfunding, and I believe these rules and proposed amendments provide smaller companies with innovative ways to raise capital and give investors the protections they need."

Following is a quick overview of Regulation Crowdfunding investing limits (for the details, go to www.sec.gov):

- **For companies seeking funding:** Can raise up to $1 million in a 12-month period

- **For individual investors:** Can annually invest a small amount if wealth is less than $100,000, or a larger amount if it exceeds $100,000

In addition, all transactions are required to take place through an SEC-registered intermediary, either a broker-dealer or a funding portal. Furthermore, there are rules for the registration of these crowdfunding portals. Companies participating in Regulation Crowdfunding must file certain information with the SEC and provide it to investors and the intermediary facilitating the offering, disclosing among other things:

- The price to the public of the securities or the method for determining the price, the target offering amount, the deadline to reach the target offering amount, and whether the company will accept investments in excess of the target offering amount;

- A discussion of the company's financial condition;

- Financial statements of the company that, depending on the amount offered and sold during a 12-month period, are accompanied by information from the company's tax returns, reviewed by an independent public accountant, or audited by an independent auditor. A company that is using this program for the first time and offering over $500,000 but not more than $1 million in securities is permitted to provide reviewed rather than audited financial statements, unless they have financial statements that have been audited by an independent auditor;

- A description of the business and use of proceeds from the offering;

- Information about officers and directors as well as owners of 20 percent or more of the company; and

- Certain related party transactions.

These are the federal rules; check your state for additional rules they have in place.

While Regulation Crowdfunding provides another source of potential funding, it comes with a range of costs: legal and accounting, audited financial statement preparation, and an annual registration fee.

The first statistics on the new program are available from Crowdfund Capital Advisors. Here is a quick summary of their report after three months of the program launch:

- 82 companies registered offerings, requesting $45.7 million

- $7.2 million in capital was committed, with average amount raised of $117,315 and $810 the average investment commitment

- The largest sectors for investment include technology—software/games, hardware—wine and spirits, food and beverage, and retail

- Three campaigns have reached the $1 million cap allowed under the regulations: a brewery, a Hollywood studio, and a diabetic medical device company

There is week-over-week increase in activity, so the results will get larger with time and experience.

Key Lessons

✓ Everyone can now invest equity in start-up and privately held companies.

✓ For individuals, there are limits to the amount of the investment based on your income.

✓ For companies, there are limits to the amount that can be raised and reporting requirements.

Have I read the regulations to know what is involved in registering my company with an SEC-approved crowd-funding portal?

Can I find someone who has done this before and learn from their experience?

How much will it cost me for an equity crowdfunding campaign?

Audit	
Legal	
Accounting and Information Systems	
Campaign Development and Associated PR	
Ongoing Investor Communications	
Other	

How much can I reasonably expect to raise?

Chapter 22

HEAVENLY FINANCING

How to Attract Angel Investors

This chapter is about angel funding, not the more commonly known source of equity financing: venture capital funding. While both may be from the same family of equity funding sources, they are very different. Venture capital (VC) is usually formed from a pool of venture capitalists' own and other funds, and investment minimums are in the $5 million to $10 million range, with a time horizon of 5 to 10 years and an expected return of 30 times the original investment. VCs often strive for the "home run"—one or two deals that will accomplish the goals of the whole fund.

Angel funding is usually from the investor's personal funds, in the $25,000 to $1 million range, and when grouped with other angel investors, an upper investment amount is about $2 million. The time horizon is typically three to seven years with an expected return of 5 to 10 times the original investment (in other words, angel funding is significant but smaller investments with more modest goals and less time to a successful outcome). If your funding needs are in the $1 million to $5 million area, that is a difficult range, so you might consider a smaller initial investment from an angel, build some accomplishments, and then undertake subsequent financing rounds at higher valuations.

According to Jeffrey Sohl, "The Angel Investor Market in 2015: A Buyers' Market," Center for Venture Research, May 25, 2015, angels invested $24.6 billion in 71,110 U.S. companies. And the "MoneyTree Report," a collaboration between PriceWaterhouseCoopers and the National Venture Capital Association, found that VCs invested $59.8 billion in 4,535 U.S. businesses.

Not only do VCs invest at different rates and amounts, but they also have different incentives (and goals)—so much so that it is not wise for an entrepreneur to mention to an angel that they are in deep discussions with a VC. You may think it will add to the legitimacy of your opportunity, but in reality, it is a turn-off to the angel funder.

Angels Defined

Angel funding comes from high-net-worth individuals who, after doing due diligence on an investment opportunity, invest their personal capital. Angels usually favor equity investments, either common or preferred shares, and on occasion will use convertible debt.

Angels operate as individuals or in groups, and if they are involved in a group, there are many operating models. In the angel group I am involved with, the due diligence is undertaken collectively. Each member votes to participate with their own capital, and a majority vote is required for a group deal. Some angels and angel groups are passive, meaning after they invest, they wait relatively silently for their return, while other groups are quite active, wanting a very direct and visible governance of their investment, which usually translates to a board seat.

In return for their investments, angels expect a 5 to 10 times return on their investment. While this might sound high, there is recognition that these early-stage company investments are risky, all will not be successful, and there is usually some ownership dilution in subsequent financing rounds. Therefore, angel funding is more expensive than bank loan financing, but for the start-up, pre-revenue, and other early-stage companies, bank funding may not be available, and if it is an option, $300,000 may be an upper limit. Especially with the more active angel groups, their membership often consists of experienced individuals who can also provide guidance and mentoring to their portfolio companies.

Equity financing involves selling a portion of ownership in your company. This ownership can be in the form of common or preferred equity—the company gets the cash and the investor receives an ownership stake. The angel investor becomes a part owner of your company in the agreed proportion to the funds provided. As angels are your partner, you want to be sure to pick the right partners.

IT'S LIKE THIS: An entrepreneur with an electronic device was at first very pleased to secure $10 million in investment from a group of doctors and dentists. With this level of funding, the investor group received two board seats. Throughout the first three years of operation, the entrepreneur-CEO typically received up to three telephone calls a day from these board members, worrying about operational details or a competitor news item that might affect the business. This excess attention to investors was taking valuable time away from marketing and other important functions, and the business stagnated.

Angels are your partner and often are not passive about it. They may sit on your board of directors and will be involved in key decisions. They are at risk just as you are—there are no guarantees to being rewarded for their investment. When they do get rewarded, angels are repaid in one of two ways. First by periodic dividends, but this is rare in a new company as all funds are used to help grow the business. The second method is by selling their shares to someone else in a subsequent financing round. Therefore, a consideration of most angel equity investors is an exit strategy in about five years but preferably less. All angels will ask you about your exit plans—when you intend to sell your company and cease involvement in your creation.

How to Secure Angel Funding

Before you start contacting local angels, you should understand what they look for so you make sure you are approaching the right angel groups and providing them with the information they need to make a "go" investment decision.

Prior to looking at the specifics of any investment opportunity, angels will determine if there is a fit with their investment thesis. Typically, angels invest in companies located within a day's drive so they can be active investors. Some angels invest in companies solely in their state or region, while others focus on certain industries or businesses in specific development stages, including women-owned businesses, military-academy graduates, clean energy, chemicals, and biotech. Some angel groups are associated with universities and invest in that school's graduates.

Find out what industries the group specializes in funding and what stage they focus on: start-up, pre-revenue generation, post-revenue generation, etc. You might also see investment stages referred to as seed, A, B, C, and D financing rounds. While not black and white, seed round usually refers to the first round of funds obtained from investors other than yourself and family and friends. It is typically for companies with less than $500,000 in sales. A, B C, and D funding rounds follow as needed and represent companies that have validated their value proposition, have market traction and established management teams, are growing at 20 to 100 percent per year, and in the later rounds are examining an exit strategy.

Then look on their website to find out how to submit an application. Often it consists of a two-page summary of your business, so a good place to start is your business plan executive summary. Some angel groups will undertake extensive due diligence at this point and only invite in to make a presentation those companies with a well-thought-out business plan that meets the group's criteria.

Another approach is used by my angel group: If we are interested in your company, we will invite you to give a 20- to 30-minute PowerPoint presentation about your business, detailing what you are looking for and why this would be a good investment. This presentation is often referred to as an investor pitch or pitch deck. A good example/template for an investor pitch deck is on Slide Share. (Go to www.slideshare.net and search for "best investor pitch deck.")

If you pass this screening stage, which is attended by a few members of the angel group, you will be asked back for a presentation to the full group. If that is successful, then extensive due diligence will start and the group will want to know everything about you and your business (historical, current, and projected). It is often the case that entrepreneurs seeking angel funding will make presentations to several angel groups to see if there is any interest.

Angels have evaluation metrics for each potential investment. High on the list is management's experience in operating and growing a company. Again, this is as much a bet on the entrepreneur as it is on the company. The product or service must be strong enough to attract a steady and growing set of paying (hopefully repeat) customers. Also high on the list is the size of the potential market and the company's ability to scale up to this level of operation. Therefore, it is not surprising that the parts of the country that have the highest concentration of angel groups (Silicon Valley, Boston, New York City, and Washington, DC) are those areas that have many IT-related start-up companies. The fourth consideration is what valuation the owner places on the company as this will determine the amount of control the owner will trade for the financing and is a key driver of the ultimate return to the angel investor(s).

Implied with the amount of return expected by angel investors and the amount of due diligence conducted is the type of business they usually invest in. Angels look for businesses that can become national in scope, reach a very wide audience, attain high margins, and create some barriers to others entering the market. There are about 650,000 new businesses started each month in the U.S., and my observation is that only about 5 percent have these characteristics. For 2015, angel investments by industry deals, according to the Angel Capital Association/Angel Resource Institute's "Halo Report," were software, 30 percent; health care, 22.9 percent; commercial services, 6.4 percent; pharma and biotech, 6.3 percent; media, 3.9 percent; energy, 3 percent; IT hardware, 2.6 percent; consumer goods and recreation, 2.4 percent; and all others, 22.6 percent.

Angels are also interested in knowing if the entrepreneurs who founded these businesses are interested in an enlarged scope of operation and if they are willing to take the personal and financial risk to obtain these goals. So if you have a successful local establishment, plan to expand just within your county or parish, are generally happy with the current level of earnings/cash flow and the lifestyle it affords you, then angel or VC funding is probably not for you.

A FACTOR OF 5

Once a fit is established, angels will look at the following five factors for each investment opportunity. While the factors are similar across angel groups, each will have its own idea on the importance given to each.

Factor 1: Management and Management Team

- Is the founder/CEO tested in the current company?

- Does he/she have a strong CV with relevant experience?

- Is the founder/CEO coachable?

- Does the founder/CEO have experience starting, growing, and exiting companies? In other words, are they a serial entrepreneur?

- Has the management team worked together before, especially in difficult situations?

- Does the management team have strong CVs with relevant experience?

Factor 2: Product or Service

- Does the product or service have a clear and tested value proposition with multiple customers?

- Does the product/service have some market traction? Is it more than just an idea?

- Are favorable customer experience references available?

Factor 3: Competitive Landscape

- What are the barriers to entry by competitors?

- Is there any enforceable intellectual property?

- How long would it take a well-heeled competitor to copy the product/service and obtain market traction?

- How many competitors exist with the company's same strengths and weaknesses?

Factor 4: Market Attractiveness

- Is the market several billion dollars strong?

- Does the company have the potential to reach about $10 million in annual sales? How long will it take?

- How much market penetration can be achieved in the first year?

Factor 5: Financials

- How long will it take the company to break even?

- What is the magnitude and stability of cash flows?

- Is the current company valuation attractive and justifiable?

- Assuming the company achieves its milestones with this investment, when and how large will the next funding be?

- Have the founders, family, and friends already invested in the company?

Increasing the Odds

Angel groups usually have limited resources for considering and reviewing requests for funding and are usually highly selective since they have limits to their funding capabilities. For instance, the angel group I am part of sees approximately 250 to 300 proposals a year and typically invests in four to six. With these odds, it behooves the entrepreneur to find someone they know or someone who knows someone in the angel group to make a personal recommendation—the classic networking approach. Companies recommended by members within an angel group could receive more attention. Entrepreneurs should also do their homework and know the angel or angel group's identity, membership, and their backgrounds before making a face-to-face presentation. Often this information is on the angel group's website.

IT'S LIKE THIS: At a recent screening session, two companies were invited to present 30-minute pitches to obtain funding interest. The first was a retail app in a very crowded niche. The founder stressed the importance of getting the app right and was not overly interested in revenues. As a result, the pitch contained no financial information—present or projected. The founder did not do his homework on what was of interest to the group, and thus, received a pleasant "thank you." The next presenter had a cyber security start-up. The founder fully researched the market, included current and projected financials, and understood his audience's interest. He walked away with a full investment commitment.

If you are not successful in obtaining funding from an angel group, it is possible that members of the group might invest individually and separate from the group if they like your product or service idea, economic potential, and your management experience.

Closing a Deal

If your initial pitch to angels attracts interest and you successfully complete the group's due diligence process as well as agreeing to the investment terms, you are ready to close the deal. This will involve much legal paperwork, and I recommend engaging a lawyer with deal transaction experience. If you are offering preferred stock, the deal documents might have titles like Preferred Stock Purchase Agreement, Amended and Restated Certificate of Incorporation, Investors' Rights Agreement, Right of First Refusal and Co-Sale Agreement, Voting Agreement, Restated Bylaws, Unanimous Written Consent of Directors in Lieu of Meeting, Written Consent of Stockholders in Lieu of Meeting, and maybe others. If you are offering a convertible note or other debt security, there will be additional closing documents.

ANGEL HUNTING

Ready to start your search? Most angel groups list their investment approach and often the names of their portfolio companies on their websites. Search for angel groups in your geographic area and in your industry. In an internet search, use "angel funds in XXX" or "angel funds in YYY (industry)." Your lawyer and accountant should also have information on angels and angel funds they have worked with. Go to www.angelcapitalassociation.org to find an angel group and read the FAQs about angel investing.

Following are resources to help you narrow you search:

- **Angel Capital Association:** This trade organization for angel groups lists members by state and accredited platforms: www.angelcapitalassociation.org

- **Angel List:** This and other such platforms connect companies seeking funding and angel investors: www.angellist.com

- **Independent Research:** Google angel groups in your state/area or angel groups investing in your business sector.

- **Referrals:** Ask your lawyer and accountant for their recommendations.

Key Lessons

✓ Know your audience by recognizing the difference between angel investors and venture capitalists and, within angel groups, what the individual or group is focused on and looking for.

✓ Angels have different investment approaches; find one that matches your situation.

✓ Provide angel investors with the information they need to make a "go" investment decision.

✓ To receive angel funding, you may need to be organized as a corporation because angels are interested in equity or equity-related investments. If so, this can be accomplished when closing the funding.

✓ Angel funding is not for every type of business or entrepreneur.

✓ By using equity funding, you will be trading partial ownership in your company for investment funds.

List your business characteristics that are attractive to an angel investor.

List the contact information for three angels or angel groups in your area.

1.

2.

3.

Who can make a personal recommendation to the angels on your behalf to consider your proposal?

How much, if any, equity in your business are you prepared to trade for financing, and what is your company's valuation?

Are you prepared to have an investor on your board of directors?

What are the possible exit strategies to merge or sell your company that are typical in your industry that you can share with an angel investor?

List management experience held by you and your management team that would be attractive to an angel investor.

Chapter 23

CONCLUSION

Are We There Yet?

Yes, we have come to the end of talking about developing a business plan—its contents, style, and uses. Hopefully, you have been an active reader and have prepared each chapter's "Your Turn" section. Congratulations! Now transfer all these specifics into a single document and draft your executive summary, remembering to clearly state what business you are in, what customer need or problem you are solving, how your solution is different than the competition, the strength of your management team, why you will be successful, and the amount of any funding being requested. Remember, the executive summary is being written with a particular reader in mind. When you have finished this draft, compare it with the good practice checklists in Section I.

Although we are finished with writing the plan, the journey for you is just beginning. Now that you have a business plan, you need to use it—take it to family/friends, a banker, or angel for funding, implement the marketing action plan steps detailed in Chapter 10, establish your legal form of organization, set up your accounting and record-keeping system,and take care of all the other details you spent time thinking about and planning for. As you will have several versions of your business plan—updates as you receive feedback and different styles for different readers—keep track of what you send to whom by giving each a version number either on the cover page or in a header on each page.

Once your business is up and running and gaining customers, making sales, and generating cash flow, it is important to set year-ahead goals and key performance factors. Convert your business plan financial projections to a monthly financial report with a budget and monthly actual results comparison as noted on page 145 in the financial chapter.

As stated at the outset of this guide, a business plan becomes dated soon after it is completed, so I suggest that after a year's experience, it is time to update, as opposed to rewrite, your plan to incorporate what you have learned.

Having been through the business planning process, you are poised for success—now go put in place what you have planned.

You've started your business; now you will be dealing with these topics more in-depth. To get a sneak peek, see the next section.

Section IV

GRADUATE LEVEL

Since writing the first edition, I continue to explore and research

topics of interest to entrepreneurs starting and growing their businesses. In

particular, I have written monthly blogs for Constant Contact, SCORE, and

more recently American Express Open Forum. I have chosen 11 of these

blog posts for chapters in this section, all of which are on subjects covered

in previous sections of the book, including setting your compensation, hiring staff, creating marketing programs, seeking advice, and most important, ensuring appropriate liquidity. Each chapter is a more in-depth look at these topics.

I have included these chapters in a separate section so they do not clutter the straight line to writing a business plan found in Sections I and II. For entrepreneurs starting a business, these subjects are a peek ahead into issues to be addressed. For entrepreneurs with established businesses, they are issues you face today.

Chapter 24

A SECOND LOOK

When Should You Review and Renew Your Business Plan?

You have written your initial plan, but a business plan is a "living" document that should be revisited and updated on a regular basis to reflect changes in your business and industry and goals you want to achieve. In this chapter, we will explore what events trigger a need to update your business plan, how updating a business plan differs from creating the original, and who should be involved in the updating process.

Do I Need to Update My Entire Plan?

Most likely, no. It depends on what trigger situations you are addressing. Almost all businesses should update the strategies and tactics in the marketing section to meet constantly changing market realities.

For example, which of your actions/activities worked well and should be continued, and which should not? If everything is working, then you are not experimenting enough—not everything will work as planned and you can only grow from the lessons learned.

If updating your plan fills you with dread, don't worry. Creating your first business plan may have been a chore, but updating a plan is easier and more fun. During your start-up, you likely had little direct experience and no track record or historical information, so many of the marketing and operational forecasts were educated guesses. Now you have some experience and a track record, and you have experimented and know what works and what doesn't. Plus, you have a year's worth of information to use as a foundation.

Situations That May Trigger a Plan Update

Business plans are "living" documents and need to be revisited every so often to ensure they are still relevant. In this way you can continue to use and benefit from the strategies and tactics.

Further, business plans are forward-looking, so they are based on estimates, which means updates are often necessary. Following are some specific situations that may be cause for you to look at updating your plan:

- **Competitors have reacted to your market entry by reducing prices for similar products, extending business hours, liberalizing their return policy, providing free shipping, etc.** You must decide whether to match their tactics or stick to your plan. In either case, your revenues will be lower, so you will need to plan a course of action. These situations may affect your plan's marketing, products and services, and operations sections, with a resultant impact on the financial section.

- **A competitor has copied your product or service.** Do you have intellectual property protection (patents, copyrights), and is it economically feasible to go after the perpetrators? If yes, there will be legal expenses, and revenues may decline with the increased competition.

- **The economy has changed (inflation, recession, unemployment rates), impacting potential customers' ability to buy your product or service.** This will negatively impact your revenues, and depending on your staffing, adjustments may be needed there as well.

- **You land a major new customer, or an existing customer cancels a big contract.** The first is good news and might require more resources than originally planned, but the latter is not good and may require a fresh approach.

- **A major vendor has cut you off or changed their terms and conditions.** For example, they previously allowed a 30-day grace period but now require cash in advance. If you are cut off, you must scramble to find a replacement. Maybe you stop buying from a vendor due to quality and dependability issues, or your business has outgrown a vendor's limited services.

- **Regulatory changes impact your business.** One potential change in many states is the imposition of sales tax on all internet sales. The possible result? Online sellers and brick-and-mortar stores with the same prices—and no competitive edge.

- **You lose a key staff member, which affects productivity.** Reduced resources means either your business must reduce its size or you need to find alternatives.

- **You are ready to take your business to the next level.** Obtaining growth funds from a bank or angel investor requires a more "sophisticated" plan. Even if you do not need additional funding, a business plan based on an estimated $50,000 business might not be adequate to support a $300,000 one, which may need additional employees, for example.

Whether one of the previous reasons dictates an update or not, make it a practice to review your business plan at least once a year and plot your activities for the coming year. Do this as part of your annual planning and budgeting process at the end of your fiscal year. If you previously had your forecast in a full year increment, this time do it quarterly, and next year monthly.

Who Should Update Your Company's Business Plan?

You probably prepared the original business plan yourself, since you were likely the only employee. If you have now grown and added staff, try to involve them so there is buy-in. That way, when it is time to implement the plan, your staff will be on board and the activities will go smoother.

Key Lessons

- ✓ External and internal events can trigger the need to update your business plan.

- ✓ Business plans should be reviewed and possibly updated at least once a year, especially for younger companies.

- ✓ Updating your business plan is more focused and "fun" than writing the original one.

- ✓ Involve staff in the updating process.

- ✓ It is never too late to create a business plan.

Chapter 25

LIMBER UP

Keep Your Business Plan Flexible

You've been working on your business plan, and it seems to have everything, including five-year projections. It covers your marketing strategy and your budget, down to your everyday coffee and a reserve fund for cash flow problems. Your business plan is like a giant jigsaw puzzle, and you know where every piece goes. But this plan is no puzzle; it's a work of art.

And, if need be, you should be ready to junk it—every business plan needs to be flexible. You can love your business plan, but you shouldn't be in love with it.

Things change. Think of how the rise of smartphones and their cameras almost killed Kodak or how Netflix vanquished Blockbuster, and you should begin to see why it's important to have a business plan that's nimble. PayPal's original mission, according to the book *Founders at Work*, was specializing in cryptology. Later, they became a company that transmitted money through a personal digital assistant. It took several more years to become the online payment system it is today. Amazon.com used to be famous for being able to deliver books to people's homes; now, they're famous for delivering anything, from streaming entertainment to restaurant delivery to toilet paper, groceries and, yes, books. And it is not just technology; foods like cupcakes are fashionable one month and not so the next.

Technology, new competition, the whims of society—any number of factors may make it necessary to update your business plan, if you want your business to stick around, and even better, grow. Following are the areas in which your business plan should be flexible:

Research and Development

You probably don't have a research and development team. You may not even have a team. And that's perfectly fine. But that doesn't mean you can't set aside a few hours every month to think about your business, and how you can improve it, and whether you're headed in the right direction. If you're never doing that, you may wind up being reactive instead of proactive, and you may even find yourself ignoring your business plan and drifting to where the currents take you. You may get lucky and drift in a direction that you would have chosen, anyway, but what if you don't?

Budget

Hopefully, you have some cash in reserve for emergencies. But you may also want that money because there's an opportunity that your business can jump on, if only you had the money.

It doesn't have to be a situation in which your entire business model changes. Maybe you're in retail, and there's a fad that suddenly seizes the public imagination. You want to stock your inventory with the item and make some easy money before the fad disappears. Or perhaps you have a small construction company, and there's some much-needed equipment that's being sold at a bargain price. The equipment would help your business immensely, and you would buy—if you had the extra cash.

Your budget won't be able to prepare for every scenario, but you'll definitely want money or have funding sources lined up, not just for the bad times but to be able to grab an opportunity.

Never Stop Changing

The best way to keep your business plan flexible is if you're continually tweaking it. You may see your business plan as a means to an end, a way to convince investors that you know what you're doing, or as a road map to show you the way forward. But like every road map, you need to look at it occasionally, or you risk getting lost.

And as noted, the world is always changing, from fads to technology to how society behaves. You shouldn't keep your business plan stored on a digital file and never look at it again. You should review it at least once a year, and twice a year would be even better. Business plans and budgets are built on assumptions and projections, and these need to be continually updated. For instance, if there are any major upheavals in your business, such as a new competitor arriving on the scene, or the economy has tanked or is vastly improving, you'll want to take another look at your business plan and see if it needs tweaking.

If you have a business plan that doesn't allow itself to be tweaked, tinkered, and teased, then maybe it is you who might be too rigid.

Key Lessons

- ✓ Make sure that you have room in your schedule for R&D, to think about where your business is headed.

- ✓ Every business plan should allow for positive and negative surprises.

- ✓ Review your business plan from time to time and never fall so in love with it that it can't be tinkered with or even overhauled.

Chapter 26

LOOKING AHEAD

How to Set Up and Maintain a Budget

You've heard the saying "you need to spend money to make money" for a reason.

Especially when you're first starting your business, you'll have a lot of initial costs that require you to spend in advance of receiving payments. For example, you buy/lease a truck to deliver goods that will be subsequently billed for and funds collected, build out a retail store before opening the doors for business, hire staff before they can produce goods or offer services, and advertise to generate leads for future sales.

In a reverse situation, a nonprofit typically has a large fundraiser at the beginning of the fiscal year, then hopes sufficient donations are received to cover expenses for the rest of the year.

A budget will help you match these early expenditures with subsequent receipts so you know what to expect, especially regarding cash availability, and thus you will know where any cash shortages need to be addressed.

Preparing a budget is usually the one time a year that a small business focuses on the year ahead rather than today's challenges. You prepare a budget as a tool to help you lead, manage, and control the operations and finances of your business. There may be secondary users of the information, like your staff, who need to understand the company's goals and progress. And if you have a bank loan, your banker will probably want to see the budget and the actual results.

What Is a Good Budget Format?

When you picture a budget, you likely see spreadsheets with many numbers. But more important than the numbers are the assumptions that drive the calculations. Therefore, the first page of your budget should be these assumptions—what products/services are being sold at what prices and volumes, and what are the key drivers for expenses, like the number of staff and locations, various marketing initiatives, etc.

In essence, you have both an operations and finance budget, and the two are closely intertwined.

There are two primary financial formats you can use: income statement and cash flow statement. If you own an established business, use both, plus any accounts receivable and inventory from the balance sheet. If you own a new business, focus on just cash flow.

These formats will help you determine how much revenue you need to cover costs and make a profit so you can pay yourself, and how much, if any, cash you will need to fund cash shortfalls. A budget will give you advance notice of when these shortfalls might occur so you can start early lining up funds to cover them, such as from personal resources, a bank loan, or a credit line.

To determine the level of detail for the budget, it should sync with your monthly reports on actual revenue and expense.

Often in a business start-up, there is not enough information to have intelligent budgets in less than a year increment. So, work toward this goal: If last year's budget was for the whole year, this year do it by quarters. Likewise, if last year was by quarter, this year go for monthly.

Where Does Budget Information Come From?

If you own an established business, you have last year's results and know where you exceeded or fell short.

This is your starting point for the current year. In your assumptions, state what market and operational changes are anticipated along with any initiatives.

Also, if you created one budget for the whole company last year, and you have a team, try slicing the budget by areas of responsibility and engage team members in helping to develop budgets for their own areas—it will help with commitment and accountability.

If you are a new business, budgeting is more challenging, as there are not ready reference points. Hopefully you prepared a business plan, and in the finance section there is a forecast. Use the first year of that forecast for your budget starting point.

Using and Maintaining a Budget

For each reporting period, usually a month, prepare a report—easy if you are using accounting software—with the actual results, the budgeted amounts, and the difference for both the current month and year to date.

Usually, the budget numbers do not change, even if there are major market or operational changes, since it is important to know what the original plan was. However, in a small early-stage company there needs to be flexibility, so I suggest looking mid-year at what has happened year to date and what is anticipated for the final six months of the year, then revise the budget as appropriate.

Budgeting Tips

Following are ideas I use in preparing budgets and which I share with my SCORE clients:

- Write down the key assumptions before spending much effort calculating all the monthly details. In other words, develop the general road map before crunching the calculator.

  - For revenue, list the major products and services you offer and the number of current and expected customers by end of the year. Most important, list the product pricing and volumes expected in the coming year. List the key components of the marketing plan that will cause these sales to occur—sales team, advertising, website, email marketing, channel partners, use of social media, etc.

  - What is important to know about these sales? For example, are there freight charges that are important to track? How about returns? If you charge sales taxes, keep these amounts separate as they are the government's money. Are they cash sales, or do you provide credit terms?

- List the three cost categories separately in your budget: variable costs (those directly associated with the production of a product like labor and materials), semi-fixed (like advertising, which can be increased or decreased over time), and fixed costs (rent, insurance, most staff, audit, etc.).

- Expenses are usually easier to forecast than sales, so provide contingencies. For example, over the year you might reduce budgeted sales by 20 percent and increase expenses by 10 percent. It is better to underpromise and overdeliver.

- While a budget can be handwritten in a notebook, it is best to use software, either created with your accounting system or with an Excel spreadsheet. Preparing a budget is an iterative process. It is unlikely you will like the results of your first try, so you will tweak the assumptions and then change the numbers accordingly. Be careful not to fool yourself by changing numbers to get desired results without changing assumptions and then testing the reality of the new assumption.

Key Lessons

✓ Budgeting helps you look a year ahead to manage and control your business, focusing on the cash received and spent. So, you will know of possible cash shortfalls well in advance.

✓ Budget in the same level of detail and format as you report actual results.

✓ Mid-year examine year-to-date results, and next six months' forecast to determine if your budget should be updated.

✓ Be conservative in budget assumptions as revenues usually take longer to achieve than planned while expenses are usually ongoing.

Chapter 27

ARE YOU LIQUID?

*Determining How Much Cash
to Keep in Reserve*

Cash is the fuel that makes a business run. You need it to pay salaries (including your own), fund marketing programs to acquire and retain new customers, invest in equipment and facilities, pay rent, buy supplies, and many more day-to-day activities.

This chapter will help you figure out how much cash to have in reserve—how much is enough. Most financial experts recommend three to six months of operating expenses, but using this for every business in every situation is misleading. To determine how much cash *you* need, you must look at the following key areas.

How Much Cash Have You Been Using?

If you're an established business owner, look at your monthly cash flow report (or go to the next paragraph if you're a start-up). This report will provide a historical and seasonal perspective. Note the cash received from sales and the cash spent. The net of these two is often referred to as the "net burn rate." For example, if you have $50,000 in sales and $30,000 in expenses, your net burn is +$20,000.

Your "gross burn rate" only takes cash expenditures into account; in our example, that's $30,000 and is the more conservative amount, since it does not assume any sales are made. Historical spending patterns are a good starting point in considering future spending plans.

How Much Cash Do You Plan to Use?

Look at the monthly cash flow projection covering the next 12 to 15 months. If you're an established owner, you can find this information in your monthly budget, or if don't have a budget, from a financial forecast created for this purpose. For start-ups, you'll find your answer in the financial section of your business plan. As you did with actual cash expenditures in the preceding paragraph, look at the sales (cash in) and expenditures (cash out) separately.

Be conservative in your forecast, as actual results often differ from what's stated in your business plan. And keep in mind that expenses are usually more predictable than revenue because many are relatively fixed, such as payroll and rent (often the two largest expense categories). And for start-ups, separate the one-time upfront costs needed before you can open your doors from your ongoing operating expenses.

For a small business, the past is not necessarily the best predictor of future needs. You need to consider the stage of your business in your forecasts.

What Stage Is Your Business In?

Are you in start-up, first year of operation, maintaining an ongoing steady business, or do you have plans to grow or make large purchases? Each of these will impact the cash forecast discussed above. While an established business may have good benchmarks, a start-up has few benchmarks and the most uncertainty, and thus should be more conservative when setting cash flow needs.

In growing businesses, accounts receivable, and maybe inventory, expand to support the increased sales. But it is often overlooked that you need cash to fuel this growth—you must spend money to generate the sale before the customer remits cash.

How Long Will It Take to Get More Cash?

Now you know your cash needs for the next 12 to 15 months. The next consideration is how long it will take to get more cash if and when it is needed. If you're funding the business from your own resources, the time is short. Getting the needed funds likely means writing a check from a bank account or selling a security from an investment account—maybe three to five days until the cash is available to use.

However, if you need a bank loan to get cash, it might take two months—one month to find a bank willing to make the loan and one more month to do the paperwork. This option assumes you have a business plan in almost-ready condition and have maintained good relations with your bank if you have an established business or on your personal account if you're in start-up mode.

Raising funds from angel investors extends the time considerably. If you go this route, count on six to nine months to prepare the business plan/investor pitch, make presentations to several angel groups to find one that is interested and a good fit, and wait while the angel group conducts its due diligence.

Once you know how much cash you've been using, how much you plan to use, and how long it will take to get it, you can determine how much cash you need to keep in the business. For example, if you plan to use a bank loan to fund your cash needs and you plan to spend $50,000 a month, then you should probably keep $100,000 in your bank account—if you have certain sales revenue occurring in these two months you can reduce the needed cash in the bank by a like amount. However, if you plan on using angel funding, then you might want to have $300,000 in your bank account.

Before approaching a bank or angel group, consider some other funding sources.

Are There Other Cash Sources?

There are many other sources of cash. For purchases, ask the vendor for credit terms or a longer period in which to pay. For sales, ask customers to pay you in a shorter time frame and offer a discount as an incentive to pay earlier. Other cash sources include increasing your credit card balances, taking out a home equity loan, borrowing from family and friends, tapping into savings and retirement accounts, leasing rather than purchasing equipment—the list goes on. It's also good practice to have a bank line of credit as a safety net—one that can be dipped into when needed.

When Is the Best Time to Seek More Cash?

A common axiom is that the best time to obtain funds is when you don't need them. Sounds counterintuitive, but during these times you aren't desperate to take the only offer made. You have time to shop for the best source, with the best terms, and you can negotiate from a position of strength.

Too Much or Too Little Cash

There are many lists of common reasons for business failures. The two items frequently near the top are undercapitalization (not enough cash) and overcapitalization (too much cash). The first reason is easy to understand. But companies can also get into trouble when they have too much cash, as they often undertake projects, hire staff, buy equipment, move to larger offices, and partake in other such expensive actions, which incur ongoing implications like fixed costs.

Often these decisions are not made with the same planning rigor when cash was tighter. If your company is fortunate enough to have "excess" cash beyond the forecasted needs, then make a distribution to the owners rather than make a decision that may have far-reaching effects.

Key Lessons

✓ Know how much cash you've spent and how much you plan to spend.

✓ Determine where you will obtain cash if and when it is needed, and how long it will take to get it.

✓ Use the first two key lessons to determine how much cash you need to retain.

✓ Understand the stage of your business to determine if modifications to historical spending patterns are needed when considering forecasts.

✓ Be conservative in your estimates; rarely do actual results match forecasts.

✓ Seek cash when you are able to explore options and negotiate from strength.

Chapter 28

PAY DAY

How Much Should I Pay Myself?

To research this chapter I performed an online search for the phrase "how much should I pay myself?" I received a staggering 61.9 million results, clearly demonstrating it is a subject of much interest. After reading some of the articles and accompanying comments, I discovered it is also a subject of much frustration.

While having the freedom to set your own salary sounds great in theory, in practice, many entrepreneurs find it is not all it's cracked up to be. Determining how much to pay yourself, when to pay yourself, and where to get the funds to pay yourself depends on a variety of factors.

Start with Your Business Structure

When you question how much to pay yourself, you are referring to the amount that appears on your W-2. In some cases, you have discretion to determine your compensation; in other situations, the IRS tax form preparation process will set the amount for you. The determining factor is your company's legal structure.

- **Sole proprietors and single-person LLCs:** Your compensation is equal to your net income as reported on line 31 of Form 1040, Schedule C ("Profit or Loss from Business"). This is your reported self-employment income. You will pay Social Security and Medicare taxes on this amount, and it is included in your overall income tax calculations. Because your compensation is the same as your income, there is no formal paycheck in this setup.

- **Multiperson LLCs:** Considered partnerships, there is no salary involved; only guaranteed compensation in the form of payments and distributions. Again, you will pay Social Security and Medicare taxes on the amounts received.

- **S and C corps:** You have compensation options—as an employee (salary and bonus) or as an owner (dividends), or a mix. With the dividend tax rate usually lower than the combined income and payroll tax rate, there is a tendency to maximize dividends and minimize payroll. The IRS is alert for this practice, so tread carefully.

  To provide "protection" if audited, you should calculate a "reasonable" compensation for your responsibilities and the amount of time you devote to the position. Research recruitment websites, newspaper want ads, salary surveys conducted by industry trade groups, and ask others in similar positions. Another "protection" is to pay yourself an amount up to the Social Security base so the government is receiving all its payroll taxes.

  In a company where you are not the majority shareholder, the board of directors will typically determine your compensation based on comparable positions in related companies. It is a best governance practice for the founder/CEO not to sit on their own company compensation committee.

What to Pay Yourself With

You pay yourself with cash in the bank. Do not confuse this with sales. Sales are not the final amount of cash available. You are paying yourself out of the net balance, which is the amount left after you deduct all your expenses, such as rent, compensation for your employees, marketing, office supplies, travel, insurance, and IT.

However, even net income is not a satisfactory target. If you give your customers 30-day terms to pay, while the sale may have been made in April, you might not collect the cash until May or June. So, cash receipts may lag sales. You can't take a salary or keep your business running profitably without cash, so keep your eye on this target.

Pay Strategies

Depending on the maturity of your company and your plans for the business, you may adopt different compensation strategies.

- **Start-up mode:** It is typical for a start-up to be cash flow negative in its early months, if not years. This results from one-time start-up expenses like buying equipment, building out a facility, stocking inventory, marketing to attract customers, building products or websites, legal and accounting costs, and rent and utility deposits. Also at start-up, there are no or few customers. As such, during these times, your compensation will be light as there are no funds to pay more. Hopefully, you had prepared a business plan, including a cash-flow forecast, so you knew the range of your compensation during this period, and if there was not enough to "live on," you have made other arrangements.

- **Lifestyle vs. ramp and sell:** If you intend to own and operate your company for many years, which is what 95 percent of entrepreneurs plan, then you will want to develop, over time, a predictable compensation plan both to meet your personal needs and be predictable for yourself and the company.

However, if you are in the 5 percent who plan to start a company, ramp up products/services and sales quickly and then sell the business, your main reward will be when you sell. In this scenario, you will have very modest compensation during the time you are ramping up the company. The good news is that the sale of the company will probably be taxed at capital gains rates, which are lower than ordinary income and payroll tax rates. Of course, while this compensation plan applies to you and other owners, your employees will need competitive compensation and benefits to attract and retain them.

- **Wait and see:** Obviously, you need cash to pay compensation, and in a start-up or growing business, the cash on hand is often very unpredictable, so you need a flexible pay calculator. You can either pay yourself a percentage of cash profits, or you can pay yourself modestly during the year and a larger amount at year-end when you know the results for the year.

What to Do with the Compensation Received

Your compensation belongs to you and not the company. So, first deposit the compensation received in your personal bank account. Then you can decide to use it for personal needs or reinvest in the company, which will take the form of providing equity or a loan.

What Am I Worth?

This is a good statistic to know as you have options to continue to work for yourself or join another team, but you will not find this number in any financial statement or wage report. Revisit the compensation information you found in your research for comparable positions. If your company does not have the cash resources to pay you this amount, you might consider working for someone else.

Key Lessons

✓ There is less flexibility in setting one's compensation than many entrepreneurs anticipate.

✓ Compensation strategies are different for start-up vs. ongoing businesses, and for business that you plan to operate for many years vs. quickly grow and sell.

✓ You need a business plan with financial forecasts to know if you will have sufficient cash to pay yourself a reasonable compensation.

Chapter 29

CALL IN THE FINANCIAL PROS

Should You Hire an Accountant?

It's easy to think of accounting or recordkeeping as a "necessary evil," created and maintained to satisfy government reporting—primarily taxes.

But the fact is that beyond being something you're required to be doing under the law, accounting and recordkeeping systems are created for you to make informed customer, marketing, pricing, and vendor-related decisions.

In this chapter, you will learn the tasks associated with a company's accounting and recordkeeping system, considerations regarding who should do the work, and the differences between an accountant and a bookkeeper.

We'll also help answer an important question: Should you hire an accountant?

Accounting Tasks

Successfully managing a small business involves managing your cash. Your accounting system is critical for knowing how much cash you have in the bank each evening and if you can meet your expected expenses.

Three general activities are required for setting up and maintaining an effective accounting and recordkeeping system.

1. **Setting up the system:** Creating a process to track transactions and make projections can be accomplished using a notebook, spreadsheets, or accounting software.

2. **Entering transactions:** Transactions entered may include sales made, cost of materials purchased, employee compensation and benefits, hours worked, rent, IT, insurance, office supplies, and other expenses paid.

3. **Reporting actual results or the projections of future results:** Reports may cover the status of potential customers, sales made, sales made where customers have not yet paid, expense comparisons with the budget and same period last year, all sorts of tax reports, financial statements, and information needed to satisfy bank loan covenants.

To Outsource or Not?

When you set up your business, one of your first decisions is to determine who should handle these accounting activities. The three choices are to do it yourself, assign someone on your team to do it, or to outsource to a bookkeeper or accountant. Often with a start-up, you are the only employee and there are limited funds available, so initially the founder frequently does all the bookkeeping.

As soon as you have sufficient discretionary funds, you can consider outsourcing the task. The key is to decide if bookkeeping is the best use of your time.

You started your business because you are good at selling, developing apps, manufacturing a product, consulting, or whatever other activities produce sales. Is it more valuable to spend your time producing sales or doing bookkeeping? Unless you are in the financial services sector, it is unlikely accounting is your strength.

If you decide to outsource, there are two types of financial professionals to consider: a certified public accountant (CPA) and a bookkeeper. Each has vastly different skills and rates, and you will want to retain both, but for different tasks.

Certified Public Accountant

A CPA has been certified by a state examining board as having met the state's legal requirements. These professionals are granted certain responsibilities by statute, such as the ability to certify financial statements, and may be held liable for professional misconduct.

Accountants, like doctors and other professionals, are both generalists and specialists. Accounting specialties include tax accounting, mergers and acquisitions, and nonprofits. You need to find the right match for your needs; at first this will mostly be general accounting work.

Depending on the market and work complexity, CPAs may charge $100 to $300 an hour. So, it makes the most sense to hire an accountant only for complex or high-value projects, such as the quarterly financial reports (especially if you are required to give these to a bank or under a government contract), tax filings, ongoing or case-specific advisory services, or the financial section of your business plan. Until your company reaches several million dollars in sales, it is more economical to outsource these tasks rather having a full-time accountant.

To find a CPA, word of mouth is best. Alternatively, check out these two sites: CPAdirectory (www.cpadirectory.com) and the National Society of Accountants (www.nsacct.org).

Bookkeeper

Performing basic, day-to-day activities is best left to a bookkeeper. These tasks include gathering employee timesheets, submitting purchase-order invoices for you to pay, collecting customer payments, preparing bank deposit statements, and entering all the transaction information into your accounting and recordkeeping system.

Depending on the market and tasks assigned, a bookkeeper charges $25 to $35 an hour. Many small businesses retain a part-time bookkeeper to help set up their accounting system and enter all the transactions, until business growth justifies a full-time position. Even if you decide to do the bookkeeping yourself, you still may want a bookkeeper to help you set up the accounting system.

Bookkeepers with knowledge of other similar businesses will know which categories of revenue and expense are typical in your industry to track and report, thus saving research time and ensuring your system is set up most effectively.

To find a bookkeeper, ask an accountant for recommendations of bookkeepers they have worked with and vetted. You can also place ads in your local paper, on Craigslist or other such forums, or go to the American Institute of Professional Bookkeepers.

Don't Outsource It and Forget It

Consider outsourcing to an accountant and/or bookkeeper if you do not have the time, skills, or inclination to do this work. However, bear in mind, this is not a situation where you hire these folks and then forget about the subject. It is your company, and the financial statements are yours. When you present the financial statements to a bank, file your tax return, submit invoices to a government procurement official, or any other such use, you will be the one signing the document.

Therefore, you will need some understanding of what is included. Review important materials and ask for explanations if anything seems unclear.

Key Lessons

✓ An accounting and recordkeeping system is mainly for you, to assist in making good decisions; it is not primarily for satisfying government reporting.

✓ When deciding whether to seek accounting assistance, consider where your time is best spent.

✓ There are substantial differences in the skills and costs of hiring an accountant or a bookkeeper, so hire each where there is the best match.

Chapter 30

DEAL OR NO DEAL?

*Trading Services for Equity
in a Start-Up*

Ellen is a founder of a law firm serving small and midsized businesses, many of which are in the start-up stage and do not have the cash to pay her fees. Ellen also has a passion for yoga and teaches at a local studio.

The yoga studio owner wants to retain Ellen for legal advice, but instead of paying cash that she doesn't have, she offers Ellen a small percentage of ownership in the business.

Should Ellen Take the Deal?

Ellen's options are to forgo the potential business, reduce fees to an amount the owner can afford, or take the business, delaying payment to an unknown date and for an unknown, but potentially larger, amount.

If Ellen decides to either decline the business or lower her price, it depends on her need for current cash flow and her time available to take on the work relative to potential customers who can pay.

But if Ellen chooses to trade fees for equity (and become an owner) in the customer's business, there are a few issues she should explore first.

Here are seven things to consider if you're thinking about trading services for equity:

1. **What is the business's financial forecast?** Ellen's ownership and eventual payout is a long-term decision, so she needs to know if the business is profitable today, and its three- to five-year financial profit forecast. Also, is there a well-thought-out business plan to support the projections? Fortunately, Ellen has some experience in the yoga business; if she did not, she should seek expert opinions. She should also look at traditional financial profitability measures as well as cash flow.

2. **What is its current financial position?** Ask for the company's financial information and the owner's tax returns to understand the studio's current financial position. If the owner is not forthright in providing this information, it is a red flag. If Ellen goes forward with the deal, there needs to be a clear understanding of her rights to company financial and operating information.

3. **How are key decisions made, and how will your investment position be protected?** Since Ellen has her own business to run, she will likely be a passive investor/owner in the yoga studio. But she should still review the studio's governance structure. In particular, she should find out how the owner's compensation is determined and approved, how she decides to obtain loans or other investors to buy equipment or grow the business, and if the business were to close down, how that decision would be made.

4. **How can you "sell," or monetize, your investment in the future?** Look at the studio's operating agreement if it is an LLC, or bylaws if it is an S or C corp to understand the procedures for selling an ownership interest. The studio may have a 10-year horizon, but if Ellen has a four-year horizon, she needs to determine how she can pull out her investment.

5. **What is your legal liability?** If the company has liabilities other than accounts payable, like lawsuits, judgments, fines, or tax delinquencies, what responsibility and liability fall on owners?

6. **What is the company's valuation?** A company valuation determines the amount of ownership. For example, if the amount of legal services provided is $50,000 and value of the company is set at $500,000, then Ellen will receive a 10 percent ownership in the company. However, if the valuation is $1 million, then Ellen receives a 5 percent stake. Usually, there is a disconnect between the founder's high valuation and an investor's, which is much lower. Sometimes, a high valuation is based on a company's customer list, but in a community with several yoga studios, that is of limited value as potential customers can move freely between studios. If the studio owns assets like the building in which it is located or has an attractive lease, that can increase valuation.

7. **How will your relationship with the owner change?** Ellen now consults with the owner to set her teaching schedule. Going forward, if Ellen becomes an investor/owner in the business she will have another, very different, relationship with the majority owner. Ellen should project how the owner will be as a partner and steward of the business; this will be a subjective evaluation based on her interactions with the owner and her assessment of the owner's operating style and approach.

An alternative to trading services for equity is trading for a loan to be paid with interest at a specific date. The research is much the same, with a focus on evaluating if the studio will have the cash at the time to pay off the loan.

While we used Ellen as an example for this post, remember, the same thinking applies to accountants, consultants, or anyone else providing a service for a fee. Make sure you're researching a business fully before agreeing to take an equity deal.

Key Lessons

✓ Trading services for equity in a customer's business substitutes current pay for future pay at an unknown time and amount.

✓ You will be a small, passive investor, so make sure the governance structure protects your interest.

✓ Determine how you can get out and monetize your investment.

Chapter 31

GIFTS IN KIND

*Should You Offer Your
Services for Free?*

The best things in life are free, everyone says. So, take that as a compliment when people ask you to give up your services, products, or time—without any compensation.

If you're in business long enough, you will get these requests from family members, friends, employees, acquaintances, and strangers for your time and resources. Maybe your child's or a nephew's school will want you to donate some products or services for a fundraiser. Maybe a nonprofit you've never heard of will ask for your help. Maybe one of your employees will ask you to sponsor his kid's soccer team and pay for uniforms and a pizza party.

To some extent, you may not mind at all, or at first. It is flattering to be sought after and asked to help a school, church, or nonprofit out. But you are in business to make a profit, so it can only help you if you think things through before agreeing—or automatically saying no—when people request you to donate your time or resources.

Generally, here's when it makes sense to offer services, products, or time for free.

When the Nonprofit Aligns with Your Company's Strengths

Let's say you have a tutoring service and a nonprofit that helps disadvantaged children came to you with a proposal that you or your employees spend a few hours a week tutoring kids from broken homes. Not that you'd want to plaster this in your marketing materials and come off as narcissistic, but whether you quietly mention it somewhere on your website or if you say nothing and some customers nonetheless learn about your good works, your donation fits in with your company's marketing message: We have a first-class tutoring service.

But if a nonprofit that rescues injured songbirds asks for your money, it's nice that you're helping, but there's no logical reason that your tutoring company should be aligned with a bird-related cause, and if there's a marketing message here, it's a bit muddled: We're a first-class tutoring service that values songbirds.

When Giving Something Away Will Attract Customers

Think of the rare gas station that lets customers fill the air in their tires for free, or the bookstore that offers free gift wrapping, or even stores that let anyone use their restrooms, whether the customers are buying anything or not. You did have to buy the tire filling machine, and there's no doubt that it takes some time to wrap gifts and clean a bathroom. But not only are you fostering goodwill among your customers for letting them have some relatively minor things for free, odds are, you may get a sale. The person who knows that they can fill their tires for free at your gas station may well turn to you for their gas, lottery tickets, and milk as well.

I remember reading about a Subway franchise in Washington, DC, that was across the street from a police station. Every Friday, they brought over a tray of sandwiches to the station. Throughout the week, the police, and everyone they told, made purchases at that Subway that likely far and away made up for the free food. Why? Because it created goodwill. I'm not saying the Subway owner didn't truly want to help the police, but regardless, it was good marketing.

Being a good neighbor to the community is a smart marketing message. You're saying: "We care, and though we are a for-profit business, we are looking out for you."

When Giving Something Away Will Create a Lot of Exposure

You need to be careful here. Writers are often asked to write for free, and the standard rejoinder is: "You can die of exposure."

Obviously, exposure can be terrific, but you must ask yourself, "Am I doing this because there *might* be exposure or because there *will* be exposure?"

If a charity that has nothing to do with your brand was holding a well-attended festival in your town, and by working with them for free, you knew that you would have a lot of potential new customers seeing your brand, you probably have a solid argument for helping them out.

But if you have a start-up approach you, arguing that they'll remember you when they hit it big, if you'll just do some severely discounted—or free—work, you have no idea if what they're promising will happen. And you should be wary if a giant corporation wants you to do work for them for free, or next to nothing, and makes the argument that by working for them, you will earn more exposure.

In this case, the marketing message you will be sending to these companies and yourself is: "I don't value the work that I do."

It may sound harsh, but even with a good cause, you should always ask yourself: What's in it for my business?

If you don't, you may not be in business for long. But if you are selective about what you give away for free, your business will likely be around for years, which is a great thing for all the future good causes you will end up helping.

Key Lessons

✓ If you're going to align your business with a charity, it's best if your company's mission dovetails with the charity's.

✓ It can be smart to give away a little something for free if you get a lot of goodwill.

✓ Giving away something because a lot of people will learn about your business can be smart or foolish, depending on the situation.

Chapter 32

WALKING THE LINE

The Do's and Don'ts of Interacting with Your Competitors

There's a smart line of dialogue in the movie *Creed*, the most recent Rocky Balboa movie, which every business owner should think about. Rocky shows the young boxer he is mentoring the mirror.

"You see this guy here?" Rocky says. "That's the toughest opponent you're ever going to have to face. I believe that's true in the ring, and I think that's true in life."

Even if you're your toughest opponent, you still must deal with other competitors, and if you don't know how, your business could easily wind up flat on its back, with the other guy triumphant.

How you handle competition depends on the market. You might have a business where if your competitors are doing well, you aren't. Or you may be in a field where there's plenty of business for all, so you are competing with yourself by constantly trying to top last quarter's performance. Regardless of where you fall, here are some do's and don'ts that every business owner should remember.

Don't Spy on the Competition

Don't hack into their computer system or be anywhere that customers aren't allowed or rifle through their papers.

Do Competitive Research

Keep tabs on your competitors by doing what any member of the public can legally do, such as following them on social media or attending a speech they might give at the chamber of commerce. You can send someone to a competitor's store to pose as a mystery shopper without going afoul of the law.

That said, there's a limit to mystery shopping a competitor. If you're taking up a lot of your competitor's time by asking a bunch of questions, or worse, stringing a salesperson along, letting them think they're going to land a big sale, only to have you or your employee walk away, that's considered sleazy. Another no-no is getting on someone's mailing list. Being part of a mass emailing list is fine, but if your competitor is mailing marketing materials to you, they are spending money and time on you. In other words, take the high road.

Do Befriend Your Competitor

If you feel it's a big enough market—maybe you have a home contracting business, and it's clear there are plenty of home improvement projects to go around, and what you do isn't going to affect another business—you and a competitor might find that when you both trade information and referrals, it ends up helping both of you.

Do Steer Clear of Antitrust Laws

There are laws governing competition. You can't engage in price fixing, where you and a competitor, for instance, agree to never sell your products or services below a certain rate. Prices should be dictated by supply and demand.

Another no-no: deciding that you're going to focus on a certain territory and your competitor another. Because then, you aren't competing. There's no reason you can't be on friendly terms and recommend a competitor call your insurance agent, who found a great health plan for your staff. But the moment you and a competitor start agreeing that your companies will never do this or you'll both only do *that*, you're probably traveling down the antitrust road.

Don't Start a Price War

In a price war, competitors continuously lower prices hoping to take market share from others. Think of gas stations with electronic street signs where price is very visible. Or a furniture store trying to sell more couches, although here it is more difficult to broadly announce the price. In a price war, the customer is the only one who benefits. Often the boost in sales is temporary, as there is a limit to the amount a customer can buy. In a price war, you are selling at lower margins, and your business health might suffer.

Sometimes sellers have a "customer price protection plan" in which they will match a lower price shown to them by the customer; this limits the number of occurrences of selling below market. As a recommended in Chapter 10, "Going to Market," a low price should not be your main competitive advantage. If you have the lowest price, a competitor can match it and then you have started a price war. Also, customers might ask what is wrong with the product if it has the lowest price. A better branding strategy is to have a quality product and features, such as store hours, delivery, return policy, friendliness of service, etc.

Do or Don't Use a Noncompete Clause
for Key Employees

I have this down for both a do and don't, because in some industries, you need to protect proprietary information as well as keep employees who leave from taking your customers with them to a competitor. On the other hand, having a noncompete might make the hiring process more difficult, and you might not attract the employees you want.

Some strategies for having the best of both situations is to limit non-competes to selected positions and put a time limit, like one year, on it.

When it comes to competition, Rocky Balboa was right. You want to compete with yourself. If you keep improving your own business, you're going to give the other guy something to worry about.

Key Lessons

- ✓ Keep tabs on your competitors, but don't spy on them.
- ✓ Be friendly with your competitors, but don't forget that you are competitors, and keep antitrust laws in mind.
- ✓ Think about whether a noncompete clause is right for your business.

Chapter 33

ADVICE ON TAP

Is a Board of Directors or Advisors Right for You?

Companies registered as an S or C corp and most nonprofits are required to have a board of directors. But even if you're registered as an LLC or a sole proprietorship, a board of directors/advisors may still be beneficial.

When you have a board of directors/advisors, it isn't just you against the world. It's you and several others with a wide range of experiences and skills against the world.

Is this the route for you? In this chapter, we discuss what you should know before you decide.

When You Have No Choice

With an S corp or C corp and many nonprofits, your state corporation/nonprofit law requires that you have a board of directors that meets a minimum required number of times a year, maintains meeting minutes, and has specific board officer positions. Your company bylaws can and often do have increased requirements. The shareholders select the board of directors.

An LLC is not required to have a board of directors but may choose to do so. Sole proprietorships have only one owner, so sole proprietors do not need a board of directors since there are no other shareholders to "protect."

In all organizational structures you can decide to have a board of advisors—and it is an excellent idea. These advisors will assist/advise you in various aspects of the business, so select these individuals in the areas where you might need help—marketing, product development, customer access, finance, technology, etc.

Role of a Board of Directors

The board of directors focuses on the big picture of running a business. They should stay out of the day-to-day affairs—that's your job—but if you're going to change your business's focus, explore a new market, or take on a new business loan, the board will have a say, and they are a good resource. Directors have a fiduciary responsibility to the company and a stewardship responsibility to all shareholders—they cannot make decisions that solely benefit themselves.

Downside of a Board of Directors

Having a board of directors takes work, which is time you could be using to start and grow your business. If the board is not managed effectively, they can get very involved in running your business and this might be more "help" than you need. In addition, as most board members are paid either in cash or stock, you will be giving up some of the company ownership. Finally, a formal board of directors is your boss; depending on ownership control they can set your compensation and can fire you.

Upsides of a Board of Directors

Your business may benefit from additional experienced professionals. If your board members represent investors, this means you could attract funds to help you grow your business, and they should be with you in future funding rounds.

Forming Your Advisory Board

Ideally, an advisory board should consist of five professionals whom you can turn to for suggestions/ideas. They will not have the same authority over your business that a formal board of directors would, and you are free to ignore their advice.

Alternatively, you might join a business networking group, seek free mentoring from SCORE, a nonprofit I think very highly of and am involved with, participate in a meetup group or CEO roundtable/ forum, or join your local chamber of commerce.

Factors to Consider

If you do form a board of directors or an advisory board, you'll want to consider several factors, including:

- **Compensation:** Typically, in small, private companies, neither the founder nor the investor directors get paid in cash, but they may receive stock options. However, independent directors are typically paid 1 percent of the company's valuation in cash, plus stock options. Nonprofit board members serve voluntarily.

  If you're forming an advisory board and have the money to pay them, you should, or at least provide stock options—they will expect it. If you are a start-up that operates on a shoestring budget, then explain that up front and hope the person you're asking to be on the advisory board will agree to provide some time to share their experience and wisdom.

- **Meeting frequency:** That's up to you and your board. In the beginning (maybe up to three years), you may want to meet once a month, or once every two months for phone meetings. After that, you might meet once a quarter. Advisory boards typically meet once a quarter or once every six months, with calls to individual members as needed for their advice.

- **Who you want on the board:** You want business leaders who have experience you don't. If you get people who know exactly what you know and think like you, what's the point?

- **Board size:** Five is a good number. If you have too few people, like one or two, you aren't getting enough opinions. If you have 10, that's too many opinions, and it is difficult to schedule meetings.

- **Your meeting agenda:** Think about what you want to discuss and send out the meeting agenda and information/presentations in advance. Also, send a monthly email updating your board on how the business is going so they stay in the loop and feel more invested in the company's success.

Key Lessons

✓ Run through the pros and cons of establishing a board of directors/advisors, or simply finding some mentors or peers you can discuss your business with.

✓ Compensate your directors or advisors, even if it's with pizza and sodas.

✓ Prepare for your meetings beforehand so you walk away from these meetings with solid strategies and answers to the questions that are keeping you up at night.

Chapter 34

HATCHING YOUR BUSINESS

Using an Incubator to Launch Your Company

Somewhere in the process of starting your business, you may have wondered if you should join an incubator.

An incubator is a place where start-up and early-stage companies can live. If your business is accepted into an incubator, you will receive resources to help you build your company. These may include office space and equipment, utilities, internet service, mentors, perhaps a receptionist to take your calls or access to discounted or free accounting services, attorneys, or other professional services. Another valuable benefit is that some incubators arrange pitch meetings, in which you can discuss your company with angel investors. There are also networking opportunities, so even if you don't find an investor, you'll likely meet numerous community business leaders who can help advance your company's goals.

In other words, you do the work of planning, building, and growing your business, and the right incubator can make it easier for you. If you're interested in joining an incubator, consider the following factors.

Not All Incubators Are Alike

No two incubators are alike; some could be a perfect fit for your business while others won't. Hopefully, if the incubator is not a good fit, it will be determined during the application process and through your due diligence by talking with company founders who have been through the program.

There are many types of incubators including for-profit and those operated by your state, county, or local university. Some incubators, especially in urban areas, are more interested in helping your business grow to improve the local economy, so they may not ask you for equity. While others, typically for-profit incubators, are motivated to find potentially successful businesses with the eventual goal of monetizing the equity they take in your company.

You also may want an accelerator, which is not an incubator, although it's close and often used interchangeably in conversation. Accelerators generally take in a business with a lot of potential and help it go from surviving to thriving. Accelerators often give start-ups investment funding (in exchange for equity) and ample access to a network of experienced professionals. These programs often last a few months and are designed to get your business up and running as quickly as possible.

You might stay in an incubator a for couple years, and if you change your business plan a few times during that period, that's OK. Incubators don't want entrepreneurs who are wafflers and daydreamers, but they recognize that many start-ups take some time to get it right. Still, one day, just as with the accelerator, your business will be deemed successful enough to "graduate"—the goal for both the company founder and the incubator.

Finding an Incubator

Incubators are easy to find, but maybe a challenge to get accepted, since there is often much competition. Start with an internet search on "incubator in XX location," then try the National Business Incubation Association or your state/county economic development department. Also, search for newspaper articles covering the best incubators in the state and look for ones that seem to be a good fit for your business.

Obviously, if you find an incubator that specializes in nurturing tech businesses, and you have a cookie shop, that isn't going to be a good fit for you. And, yes, there are incubators that offer commercial kitchens for entrepreneurs who want to get their food businesses up and running.

Before you determine if an incubator you like is a good fit, make sure it's conveniently located, read its website, and research its application process, track record of successful graduates, and fees.

It Comes Down to Your Business Plan

While incubators have a reputation for being more interested in the entrepreneur's character than the actual business (because, as noted, maybe your company's focus will change), the reality is, you need a strong business plan. With competition being stiff, you can't just apply and hope everyone will notice how driven and intelligent you are. You need to write a formidable business plan that can successfully compete.

Then when accepted, if your business plan needs work, your mentors can help you refine it. But you'll never get in if your business plan doesn't show much potential and promise.

Key Lessons

✓ Do your research. Not all incubators are alike.

✓ Finding an incubator isn't hard; getting into one is.

✓ Your key to getting in is a solid business plan.

GLOSSARY

Accredited Investor: Within securities law, companies may sell shares to accredited investors without registering those shares with the Securities and Exchange Commission. There are eight criteria for qualifying as an accredited investor. The two of most interest are: 1) a person with a net worth exceeding $1 million but not including principal residence and 2) a person with an annual income of more than $200,000 in each of the two most recent years, $300,000 if jointly with spouse, and with a reasonable expectation that that will occur again in the current year.

Accounts Payable: Money that a company owes to vendors for products and services purchased on credit. Most usually the time to pay is less than a year and thus accounts payable is included on the balance sheet in the current liabilities section for those companies using accrual accounting.

Accounts Receivable: Money that a customer owes to the company for products and services sold on credit. Most usually the time to pay is less than a year and thus accounts receivable is included on the balance sheet in the current assets section for those companies using accrual accounting.

Accrual Basis Accounting: Accounting method that recognizes and reports revenues when earned (when the work is done and title and/or possession is transferred to customer) and expenses when incurred (even if the item is not yet paid for). See *cash basis accounting* for the other accounting method.

Angel Investor: An individual, alone or in a group, who provides capital to start-ups or early-stage companies. Angels are usually accredited investors and may have a personal stake in the success of the venture. These investments are characterized by high levels of risk and a compensating, potentially large return on the investment. Investments are usually local to the investor and in the range of $50,000 to $2 million.

Annual Recurring Revenue (ARR): A measure of the predicable and recurring sales revenue often used by companies with online subscription businesses (software as a service or SaaS type company). If you divide the ARR by 12, you get the Monthly Recurring Revenue, or MRR.

Balance Sheet: One of three principal financial statements (see *income statement* and *cash flow statement* for the other two) that shows at a single point in time the company's financial condition by listing its assets (what is owned), liabilities (what is owed), and net worth (the difference between owned and owing).

Break-Even Analysis: A calculation of the approximate sales volume, or other operating metric, required to just cover costs, with less volume generating a loss and more volume generating a profit. Break-even analysis focuses on the relationship of revenues with fixed and variable costs.

Budget: A forecast, usually one year's worth, of the company's income (details revenue and expense) or cash flow (details the sources and uses of cash).

Burn Rate: See *run rate*.

C Corp: A legal company formation that completely separates the company from its owners. A C corporation is considered a person and pays taxes directly to the IRS and states in which it operates. A C corporation can include "Inc." in the company name.

Cash Basis Accounting: An accounting method that recognizes and reports revenues when the customer payment is received (independent of when the customer took possession of the product or service) and expenses when paid. When the cash moves, the business event is recognized.

Cash Flow Statement: One of three principal financial statements (see *income statement* and *balance sheet* for the other two) that shows for a given period of time the sources and uses of cash and the net amount generated or withdrawn in the period.

COGS: Cost of goods sold.

Debt: An amount owed for funds borrowed that implies intent to pay back the amount, with the possibility of interest, according to an agreed-upon schedule.

Due Diligence: The investigation into the details of a potential investment, such as an examination of operations, management, financial projections, and the verification of material facts to ensure a complete understanding of the company.

Entrepreneur: A person who starts and/or operates a business.

Equity: 1) Ownership interest in a corporation in the form of common or preferred stock, or 2) balance sheet entry that equates to total assets minus total liabilities and sometimes is also called net worth.

Financial Ratios: Numeric calculations based on the company's financial statement information that helps business owners' judge their performance in many different categories.

Income Statement: One of three principal financial statements (see *cash flow statement* and *balance sheet* for the other two) that shows for a given period of time the revenues earned and expenses incurred to generate the revenue with the resultant net income or loss.

Leverage (alias Leverage Ratio, Debt to Equity Ratio): Amount of company debt divided by amount of company equity. A ratio often used by bankers to determine maximum loan size; 3:1 is a common benchmark. For example, if you have $100,000 invested in your company, the maximum loan obtainable might be $300,000.

Liquidity (alias Debt Service Coverage Ratio, Debt Coverage Ratio): Amount of cash available to pay loan principal and interest. Calculate by dividing annual cash flow after all expenses by annual loan principal and interest. Bankers use this along with leverage to determine maximum loan amounts; 1.2+ is a common benchmark. A ratio of 1 means there is sufficient cash to pay these amounts; a business that is cash flow negative would not meet this benchmark.

LLC (Limited Liability Company): A legal formation in which the owners receive the liability protection of a C or S corporation without having to conform with all the governance administrative provisions of the C corporation or the ownership restrictions of the S corporation.

Nonprofit: A corporation formed for usually educational or charitable reasons from which the owners do not benefit financially and for which a donor contribution is often tax deductible.

Run Rate: The amount of cash used typically in a month's time. This can be on a gross basis (the amount of cash spent) or on a net basis (cash spent less revenues received). This measure is commonly used when companies have more expenses than revenue.

S Corp: A legal form of corporation with ownership limitations specified by the IRS that enjoys the benefits of incorporation but is taxed as a partnership. It is sometimes called a subchapter S corporation.

SBA (Small Business Administration): Federal government agency with the responsibility to aid, counsel, assist, and protect the interests of small business concerns; to preserve free competitive enterprise; and to maintain and strengthen the overall economy of our nation.

SBDC (Small Business Development Center): Centers that provide a wide array of technical assistance and free, one-on-one counseling to small businesses. Organized by state, SBDCs have full-time staffs and are funded by the SBA, with matching funds from local host institutions, often colleges or universities.

SCORE: A nonprofit association dedicated to helping small businesses get off the ground, grow, and achieve their goals through education and mentorship. SCORE has a network of 340 chapter offices throughout the country staffed by about 12,000 volunteers.

Small Business: A business that fits the definition provided by the SBA, which sizes companies by the amount of their revenues and/or number of employees. See www.sba.gov/content/what-sbas-definition-small-business-concern.

Sole Proprietorship: The default form of company organization. If you have not applied for any other business form (for example, LLC, C or S corporation), then you have a sole proprietorship. In this business structure, the individual and company are considered a single entity.

Strategic Plan: Document and process for determining a company's long-term goals and the best approach for achieving those goals. A nonprofit business plan is often called a strategic plan since it includes information on mission and vision.

Term Sheet: A document containing the major terms and conditions under which an investment is being made. Once agreed to by the company and investor, legal agreements are prepared with all the details. Typical terms in an angel equity investment include size of offering, minimum amount needed to close, expected closing date, valuation, price per share, liquidation preferences, anti-dilution provisions, voting rights, board participation, and much more.

Value Proposition: A statement that summarizes why a consumer should buy a product or use a service that helps convince a potential consumer that one particular product or service will add more value or solve a problem better than other similar offerings. From the customer's perspective, you are answering "what's in it for me?" with your value proposition.

Venture Capital Fund: Monies invested in start-up firms and existing small businesses seeking exceptional growth potential, with managerial and technical expertise provided to the companies. Investments are usually $5 million or more.

ACKNOWLEDGMENTS

Editor: This book could not have been completed without Marla Markman's great assistance. She, of course, provided excellent editorial assistance. But more important, with her experience with entrepreneurial publications and business plan texts, she knows my target audience and provided insightful direction to make sure the message was on point to this group—the same advice I make for writing your business plan for a target audience. In addition, she knows the 101 steps needed to successfully bring a book to market and she kept me focused and on track.

SCORE Mentors: Ed Coleman, Lou Davenport, Fred Glave, Jerry Glenn, John Hocker, Ralph Johanson, Som Karemchetty, Dan Nickell, Ron Paulson, Mohan Pherwani, Dee Rogers, Richard Rose, Alan Rosenberg, and Jeanne Rossomme, Karen Williams, and Ira Wolpert. These great folks and all the Washington, DC, SCORE chapter mentors contribute their time and energy to help entrepreneurs start up and grow their for-profit and nonprofit businesses. They also took the time to read drafts of this book and provide candid feedback.

Dear Friends: Bob Rubin, Tom Pyke, and Charles Yulish provided encouragement to undertake the book-writing experience and encouragement along the way to provide entrepreneurs good insights into preparing business plans.

Ken Yancey, CEO of the SCORE Association and Foundation, brings exceptional leadership to the 10,000-plus volunteers who provide entrepreneurial mentoring and training. With a focus on business formation and job creation, Ken helps ensure SCORE is relevant to our local communities. He also has his eye on the future, including how the next wave of entrepreneurs, the Millennials, will most effectively receive all the advice SCORE has to offer.

ABOUT THE AUTHOR

Hal Shelton is a seasoned executive with more than 45 years of experience with corporations, nonprofits, and investment organizations. He uses his knowledge and expertise to help small businesses.

Currently, Hal is a volunteer with the SCORE Association, a nationwide nonprofit that provides education and training to entrepreneurs to successfully start and grow their small businesses. As a certified SCORE mentor, Hal helps small businesses take advantage of new business opportunities, develop business plans, and find and qualify for financing, with the goal of increasing the business's value and adding jobs. He also serves on the national SCORE board of directors.

Hal is also currently a member of Blu Venture Investors (BVI). This active angel investing group supports early-stage entrepreneurs in the Mid-Atlantic Region, with a primary focus on technology companies. Hal serves on the board of directors for two of BVI's portfolio companies.

Previously, Hal was senior vice president and CFO of USEC Inc., the world's leading provider of enriched uranium fuel for commercial nuclear power plants. Hal quarterbacked USEC's $3 billion privatization via an IPO, the largest privatization of a U.S. government activity. Prior to USEC, Hal held senior financial management positions with Sunoco Inc. In addition, he was on the board of directors of RWD Technologies Inc. where he was chairman of the Audit Committee as well as the Special Committee in a successful "going private" transaction. For nonprofits, Hal served on the board and as

CFO/treasurer of Mercy Health Clinic, a "safety net" organization providing free medical care and medicine to uninsured, low-income residents in Montgomery County, Maryland.

Hal holds a bachelor of science from Carnegie Mellon University, an MBA from the University of Chicago, and an honors diploma from the University of Vienna, Austria.

INDEX